How To Negotiate Physician Contracts

DEAN E. GRANT

Contracts with hospital-based physicians cost the public millions of unnecessary dollars; it doesn't have to happen if administrators and trustees know what to do.

teach'em inc.

Library of Congress Catalog Card Number:
79-66018

International Standard Book Number:
0-931028-10-8

Second printing, 1981

Cover Design by Phillip Gill

Typography and Assembly by Accent Graphics, Chicago, Ill.

Printed in the United States of America

teach 'em inc.
160 East Illinois Street
Chicago, Illinois 60611

To

Deanna and Don

who went fatherless

for Christmas, 1978

Acknowledgments:

My gratitude to the many people who encouraged me to go forward with this sensitive and sometimes provocative subject, but most of all to my secretaries, Barbara Gongaware and Ceil Furio, who persevered through all this; and Bruce Fisher, C.P.A., Neil Bennett, Richard Risk, Stephen Skorcz, Jerry Capizzi, Fred Leyva, Mark Olson, LL.B., John B. Taylor, M.D., Terence Carden, M.D., and Peter Laubach, D.B.A., for their good counsel.

Table of Contents

THE ISSUES

1. Overview — A Gordian Knot?

I have yet to see any problem, however complicated, which when you looked at it in the right way did not become still more complicated.

.....Poul Anderson

Why does a simple undertaking like physician contract negotiations pose any serious difficulties? After all, physicians and hospital leaders are reasonable people, working together for a common goal — improved health care for their patients. And it is hard to imagine that even the most complex working relationships could not be reduced, somehow, to some fundamental issues that could be incorporated into a working agreement. It is simple in theory, but unfortunately a Gordian knot in reality when applied to doctors and hospitals.

Unknown to the general public until only recently is a long-standing feud between hospitals and hospital-based physicians over the contractual arrangements and methods of compensation with these specialists. For a whole series of complicated and now regrettable reasons, many hospitals have allowed most of their hospital-based specialists to operate with open ended contracts which at best can be described as lacking common logic and basic economic principles. Predictable abuses have developed, and the public that the hospitals and the physicians serve has become increasingly outraged at these strange agreements that allow a pathologist or radiologist or other hospital-based physicians to earn exorbitant personal incomes, as the following reports indicate.

1. August 1966, a senior official of H.E.W., in reference to implementation of the Medicare Act, said, "We have received more mail on hospital-based specialist services than any other part of the program and some of the views were so strong they probably were written on asbestos paper." The most complicated single problem in the implementation of the massive

1965 Medicare program related to compensation methods for hospital-based physicians, according to noted economics professors Herman and Anne Somers in their Brookings Institution publication *Medicare and the Hospitals — Issues and Prospects.*

2. The chief executive officer, medical director and associate administrator of a hospital in Michigan resigned in 1968 when the hospital's radiologists refused to accept any upper limits on their compensation contract with the hospital, and in the resulting crunch, the hospital's trustees did not support administration's position. Said the hospital's medical administrator, Dr. Kenneth Williams, "All we were trying to say was, how can you go on spiraling into six figures? . . . These types of situations that I describe as scandalous — where pathologists, radiologists and other hospital-based physicians have exorbitant contracts — exist only because the hospital trustees and management allow them to exist. . . . I'm working for the patient and I have a public charge!"

3. *Washington Post,* November 1, 1972, headline in a six-part series: PATHOLOGISTS MAKING $200,000 A YEAR, "This favorable arrangement with pathologists and radiologists . . . is one of the many illustrations why it costs $170 a day to be hospitalized at an institution like the Washington Hospital Medical Center and why hospital costs are rising at about four times the rate of other consumer prices since 1965 . . . Testimony before the Senate Anti-Trust and Monopoly Subcommittee, a 1967 Justice Department suit against the pathologists revealed . . . That pathologists and other hospital medical specialists have a monopoly on the services they offer, and they use it to force hospitals to give them an unusual form of compensation."

4. February 4, 1973, a *Detroit Press* editorial headlined as MEDICINE'S NEW ROYALISTS: "'If I were to tackle this job [renegotiating a hospital-based physician contract], I would probably lose my entire career," said the administrator of a prestigious 500 bed hospital in Detroit. "That's how powerful these guys are.'"

5. *Modern Healthcare,* September 1976: John Alexander

McMahon, president of the American Hospital Association, in response to Sen. Herman Talmadge's Senate Health Subcommittee's negative conclusions about open ended hospital-based percentage compensation arrangements was quoted as saying, "This is an isolated problem in some cases . . . most pathologists get an appropriate compensation in line with other physicians."

6. Dr. Sidney Wolfe, director of Ralph Nader's Health Research Group, cited a 1977 HEW report indicating that pathologists and radiologists with the most common open ended contracts (percentage of departmental revenues) earned incomes more than twice those of their salaried counterparts, and the Nader report concluded that these open end contracts add $215 million annually to patient bills.

7. July 1977: Senate Finance Committee's Sub-Committee on Health hears testimony relative to the Medicare and Medicaid Reimbursement Reform Act that annual payments to hospital-based specialists amounted to as much as $500,000.

8. *Chicago Tribune,* August 16, 1977, editorial, RALPH NADER v. THE HOSPITALS: "The special treatment involved here smacks of a boondoggle . . . if the hospitals and specialists' associations involved feel that there is an advantage for the public in their cozy arrangements, let them explain it. If not, they should work together — joined by insurance companies — to end it. There are enough causes of rising costs which hospitals can't control; their sincerity will be enhanced if they do all they can to hold down the costs they can control."

9. New York Governor Hugh Carey, announced a list of health care priorities for his administration in 1978, and this list specifically included a plan for the elimination of the commonest hospital-based physician compensation method, *i.e.* the percentage of revenue arrangement.

10. *The Sun,* August 28, 1978, article headline: HOSPITAL PAY BRINGS END TO AID . . . "Angered by information that Union Hospital of Cecil County pays one physician who handles pathology and nuclear medicine $433,000 a year, the hospital's largest auxiliary group has balked at raising further funds ($150,000) for the hospital . . . The Treasurer of the hospital's

Auxiliary was quoted: 'This is a phenomenal salary. . .but our prime concern is how it happened. How did it reach this proportion before it was picked up? This is administration? This to us is mismanagement of funds.'"

11. May 3, 1979, *Wall Street Journal*. Responding to an editorial in the *Wall Street Journal,* Sen. Herman E. Talmadge of Georgia wrote: "My bill. . .would establish a test for reasonableness for the commissions that some pathologists charge for tests performed by hospital technicians. . . .These commissions which are based on the work of other people often bear no relationship to the time and effort the pathologist himself actually expends in supervising the laboratory. A study prepared for HEW by Arthur Andersen and Company indicates that almost one-third of the pathologists who were paid on this commission basis received more than $150,000 in 1975."

Hundreds of similar disclosures could be cited about this issue and they all have the same basic flavor. What is important, however, is that the conflict over these unique compensation arrangements between hospital-based physicians and hospitals is not new; it has been a real issue from the mid-1960's to the present. Also, it is not localized to one area of the country or to just a few specific hospitals; nor has it been a problem with pathologists only, but has involved radiologists and other hospital-based physicians.

Furthermore, the problem has not come to light through an accidental, one-time news media expose nor has it been the pet lament of just hospital administrators. Quite the contrary; in spite of frustration felt by most hospital administrators over this issue and the explicit denial of the existence of a serious problem by the American Hospital Association, expressions of outrage over these contracts have come from the news media, consumer action groups, regulatory agencies, federal and state elected officials and in one case even a hospital's auxiliary.

Any issue that can generate so much public concern, that can result in terminations and resignations of hospital administrators, that can cause an endless series of special Congressional committee investigations and that can even stymie the monumental Medicare Act — such an issue certainly warrants careful examination.

To make it possible to negotiate away from these contracts, we must be aware of all the issues that surround the real problem so we can effectively negate or at least neutralize the arguments that are frequently used to make the problem appear so unfathomable that it is best left alone.

Underlying the difficulties between hospitals and hospital-based physicians is the fact that the relationship between physicians and hospitals, in general, is very confusing and complex. Is a hospitalized patient the patient of the admitting physician or is he a patient of the hospital? Who is ultimately responsible for the quality of medical care a physician practices in the hospital — the hospital or the physician himself? Does the physician in private practice have any informal contract with the hospital and what are the reciprocal responsibilities of these contractors? And there are many more. In 7,000 hospitals throughout the United States such questions are being asked in one way or another and unless some reasonable answers come forth, this inherent conflict between hospitals and doctors can have disastrous consequences for this industry some time in the early 1980's.

Although we cannot hope to solve this broad problem quickly, effective contract negotiations with hospital-based physicians might help us test the bigger issue. The hospital-based physician, after all, is already the medical profession's organizational and functional amphibian — partly absorbed into the hospital structure while simultaneously retaining, though obviously under some duress, the professional independence and freedom of the medical profession as a whole. In a sense the hospital-based physician may also be viewed as the medical profession's first assigned line of defense to test its ability to resist the stress of hospital intrusions into the practice of medicine. In effect, then, the whole contract dispute between hospitals and hospital-based physicians may not be the real issue at all. But at least it is a tangible one on which administrators, trustees and physicians can get a solid hold and this is the context in which the issue will be presented in this chapter.

Hospital administrators and trustees do not need instruction from me on the meaning of "hospital-based physician." However, a review of the four basic categories of physicians who have formal or informal contracts of service with a hospital should help clarify some of the issues that arise. If it does nothing else it will serve to emphasize the number and diversity of specialties and sub-specialties involved, each one of which poses its own special problems.

The two most important are those that provide some clinical, diagnostic or therapeutic service and those that provide medical administrative services in the hospital. The other categories would include academic physicians with teaching responsibilities, and interns and residents in postgraduate training programs.

The first of these four categories includes pathologists, radiologists, radiation therapists, nuclear medicine physicians, emergency care physicians, neonatologists, anesthesiologists, psychiatrists, nephrologists, contracted surgical assistants, employee health physicians and hospital medical "house officers," as well as those physicians responsible for such specific diagnostic and interpretive services as the following: electrocardiograms, echocardiograms, electromyleograms, electroencephalograms and pulmonary function tests among others. In the second category, hospital-based physicians who are appointed to fulfill medical administrative functions under contract include the medical director (or director of medical affairs), the director of medical education, clinical department chairmen (e.g. for the departments of medicine, surgery, pediatrics, psychiatry, etc.), various medical directors or medical coordinators of specialty units and professional departments including intensive/coronary care units, operating and recovery rooms, respiratory care department, EKG and EEG departments, cardiac catheterization laboratory, alcohol treatment unit.

A hospital-based physician may overlap into several categories, as for example when the director or chairman of emergency medicine has both a clinical responsibility to render some of the emergency care services while also being responsible for the medical administration, coordination and medical policy-making of this department. So, too, a cardiologist may perform EKG interpretations and also be responsible for the administrative direction of the EKG Department.

In addition, more and more appointed medical staff committee chairmen are being paid by the hospital for such duties and these physicians would fall into the medical administrative category of hospital-based physician services. For example, the appointed chairman of the utilization review committee, who also may be titled "medical coordinator of utilization review"; again the chairman of the continuing medical education committee may also serve as coordinator of medical education in lieu of a full-time director of medical education.

Other categories of hospital-based physicians have not been listed in detail because their role in community hospital settings is limited; these include university-hospital medical educators (professors), medical researchers, interns and resident house-staff, and physicians employed by federal, state and municipal hospitals.

What all these hospital-based physicians have in common is some kind of formal or informal contractual relationship with the hospital to provide certain specific services in or for the hospital, whether part time or full time and whether it involves salaries (or other fixed payments) by the hospital or other arrangements for compensation for these services, such as percentage of the departmental revenues, payment per unit of service performed, or hours of service provided. Even a physician who leases space from the hospital, as for example a nephrologist who operates a renal dialysis unit, can be classified as a hospital-based physician because he needs some contractual relationship and approval by the hospital to provide this particular service.

My definition of the "hospital-based physician" is somewhat broader than the more traditional one that is usually confined to a physician who practices in the hospital exclusively and who has a financial arrangement with the hospital. The problem with the more restrictive definition is that it does not take account of the many physicians who have formal or informal contracts for service with the hospital, but whose practice is not confined exclusively to hospital services. For example, internists/cardiologists are frequently reimbursed by the hospital for EKG interpretations even though these physicians retain private practices of medicine and cardiology as well. Likewise, an internist specializing in chest medicine may also receive compensation from the hospital for interpretations of pulmonary function tests, but this may not be his sole practice. Based on a 1973 A.H.A. survey, half of all U.S. hospitals had contracts with internists for such specific services in cardiology and other areas. This group represents a sizeable number of physicians who should be included in this definition.

In addition, there are many circumstances in which an anesthesiologist, pathologist or radiologist may have only a part-time commitment to a hospital and may spend the rest of his time practicing at other non-hospital institutions such as a free-standing surgical center, a private laboratory or a private x-ray facility. Also, an appointed part-time clinical department chief may devote only a quarter or half of his time to the hospital and the remainder to his own private practice of medicine. For our purpose, all these physicians will be considered under the definition of hospital-based physicians to the extent that they have some formal or informal contractual relationship with the hospital for some specific services.

In some cases a physician may not receive direct financial compensation from the hospital for his services, but rather bills patients directly. They also should legitimately be considered hospital-based because there is an implied contract of exclusive franchise or monopoly between the hospital and these physicians. So it does not really matter whether the hospital pays the physician directly or allows him the exclusive privilege of providing the service and billing the patient directly. This frequently happens with anesthesiologists and is occurring more frequently with radiologists and other specialists.

In a comprehensive 1973 survey by the American Hospital Association, its study director, Marian Kessler, reported that among all community hospitals in the United States there was an average of 19.2 physicians under contract with their hospitals; roughly 80,000 physicians throughout the country are affiliated with hospitals through some contractual basis that involves remuneration from the hospital for some or all of their services.

This figure was, in fact, conservative because it did not even include several other hospital-based physicians who do not have a direct remuneration contract with the hospital, *i.e.* those radiologists, anesthesiologists, nephrologists, and others who define themselves as independent contractors and bill patients directly. To include these would raise the total estimate of hospital-based physicians in this country to almost 100,000 in 1973. The Kessler study also revealed that between 1972 and 1973 alone there was an 18.9 percent increase in the average number of contract physicians per hospital, and at this annual rate it can be concluded that the number of hospital-based physicians in the United States is now substantially more than 100,000 — especially in light of the more recent developments in the following areas:

1. The growing need for organized hospital continuing medical programs to help physicians meet new state relicensure requirements.

2. The need for more medical administrative direction in the quality control auditing and utilization review process in compliance with the P.S.R.O. provision of PL 92-603.

3. The increasing insistence on greater medical care accountability ensured by board-appointed medical administrators and clinical departmental chairmen resulting from the Darling *v.* Charleston Memorial Hospital case, the Nork case, and other judicial decisions that have found hospitals negligent for their failure to ensure adherence by medical staffs to approved standards of care.

4. The whole new breed of hospital-based medical specialists who are now arising in response to the medical technology explosion, including those involved in nuclear medicine, ultrasound, thermography, and computerized axial tomography.

5. The increasing demand for ambulatory care specialists, including emergency physicians and hospital-based outpatient specialists in response to the legislative encouragement of vertical care services under P.L. 93-641, the National Health Planning and Resources Development Act.

Although it might be expected that each group of hospital-based specialists would have a unique contractual relationship with the hospital, consistent with their own specific services, there are, in fact, only seven basic contracts and methods of compensation used by all types of hospital-based physicians. While there are wide variations in the terms of the contracts, a brief summary of the seven commonest methods of compensation will suffice at this point.

1. Salary. This is either a fixed payment to the physician as an employee or a nonpayroll contract payment (such as would be made to a hospital-based physician who has incorporated himself.)

2. Percent of Gross Charges or Gross Income. This simply means the hospital-based physician receives a negotiated percentage of the gross billings or income of the department (frequently about 25 percent for pathologists and 33 percent for radiologists). Three common types are: simple percent of gross with or without routine deductions for certain allowances, discounts, etc.; percent of gross income with an upper limit on earnings; percent of gross income with sliding scale (*i.e.* varying percent based on volume of services).

3. Percent of Net Income (with the same three common variations as those listed above). Like Percent of Gross, this simply means the hospital-based physician receives a negotiated percentage of the department's income, but with the additional proviso that it is based on the net income (or profits) of the department, after deductions for the costs of operating the department.

4. Fee-for-Service (based on relative value index, area-wide averages, or other means of charge determination). This simply refers to a professional payment per procedure, and what this fee is and who bills for it is subject to negotiation. Two ways this billing can occur are:

4.1 Direct billing of patients by the hospital-based physician on a fee-for-service basis. This is sometimes called "Separate Billing" (See Note on Page 12).

4.2 Combined billing of the patient by the hospital for both a hospital and physician component, with the hospital reimbursing the specialist for the portion of professional fees collected.

Note: The term "Separate Billing" has been the source of some confusion. It usually, but not always, has been synonymous with direct billing, implying that separate billing means that the bill the physician submits to the patient is separated from the bill the hospital directly submits to the patient. To avoid confusion "Combined Billing" will be used here in the sense that a single bill is sent by the hospital for both the professional and hospital component, whether or not the bill itself shows a segregation of the two components.

5. Lease Arrangements. The physician leases the space and/or equipment from the hospital and, typically, but not always, employs the technical, nursing and clinical staff himself. The hospital may or may not bill the patients on behalf of the hospital-based physician in this arrangement.

6. Minimum Income Guarantees. Under this arrangement the hospital assures the hospital-based physician a minimum income independent of the volume of services provided, and the physician might also use any of the other compensation arrangements already listed.

7. Combinations of 1 through 6. This could, for example, include a basic salary to the pathologist for all routine laboratory work plus a fee-for-service arrangement for all autopsies and surgical pathology procedures he has to perform and interpret.

I believe that all but two of these contracts/compensation methods are open ended and ultimately yield inequitable levels of compensation that may have little relation to the work effort or skills of the physicians who provide these services. The salary arrangement and the combined billing arrangement (with hospital approval of both the charge structure and number of hospital-based physicians required) are the only two contractual arrangements that are not open ended or otherwise allow compensation for work that is not actually performed.

Two of the other types of contracts, in particular, are worth exploring in depth because they reveal the fundamental problems and abuses inherent in virtually all such relationships between the hospital and the hospital-based physicians. One involves the so-called percentage of revenue arrangements wherein the physician shares in the gross or net revenues or billings generated by the hospital department. The other contract is direct billing which allows the hospital-based physicians, rather than the hospital, to bill patients (at fees frequently determined by the physician alone).

These two types of contract are the most prevalent, for reasons that will soon be obvious, and are most consistently used by pathologists, radiologists and anesthesiologists. In a 1972 study by A. T. Kearney, management consultants, it was found that 62 percent of all hospital-based radiologists were on a percentage of gross or net arrangement and another 29 percent were on a fee-for-service arrangement (either direct billing or combined billing). Only 6 percent were receiving straight salaries. In this same year 52 percent of pathologists were on percentage of revenue arrangements, and 28 percent were using fee-for-service; 17 percent were salaried. The majority (64 percent) of anesthesiologists bill patients directly on a fee-for-service basis.

2. Financial Impact

Until early 1978 no one knew for sure the real financial consequences of the prevalent use of these two common types of contracts, though most hospital administrators understood how out of control the situation had become, even if they were reluctant to admit it. In late 1977, the Department of Health, Education and Welfare's Health Care Financing Administration division released a shocking 250 page report on the results of its 1975 study of contracts between hospitals and hospital-based physicians.

The report, entitled *Study of Reimbursement and Practice Arrangements of Provider-Based Physicians,* disclosed the following average annual earnings for 1975: hospital radiologists — $103,200; hospital pathologists — $98,400; anesthesiologists - $80,000. More significant is the fact that the study revealed once and for all that the personal incomes of hospital-based physicians vary dramatically depending upon the type of compensation arrangement they had negotiated with the hospital, thereby demonstrating the importance of negotiating reasonable contracts. Salaried radiologists earned $52,600 compared to $124,400 for their fellow radiologists who had percentage of revenue arrangements. An even more dramatic situation was noted with pathologists. Those who worked on a percentage of revenue basis earned almost three times more than other pathologists. In this 1975 study, the revenue sharing pathologists had earnings of $138,200 while their salaried counterparts earned only $49,200.

Almost a third of all pathologists and radiologists who were on percentage of revenue arrangements earned in excess of $150,000 in 1975. This is a remarkable figure, especially since it could mean just about anything over $150,000 and also because it meant these physicians were earning more than 15 times the median net income ($10,000) for all full time employees in the United States in 1975. By a little extrapolation, based on the fact that more than 50 percent of pathologists and radiologists are on percentage of revenue arrangements, we can then estimate that in 1975 approximately 1,200 community hospitals allowed about 4,000 of their radiologists and pathologists to earn personal incomes in excess of $150,000.

This certainly does not seem like an isolated situation as was suggested by the President of the American Hospital Association in his 1976 response to Sen. Herman Talmadge's Senate Health Subcommittee's opposition to percentage of revenue arrangements. Nor for that matter is it easy to concur with the American Hospital Association's position that "most pathologists get an appropriate compensation in line with other physicians," especially when a report of the Council on Wage and Price Stability revealed that for 1976 the median personal income for all self-employed, fee-for-service physicians in this country was $62,799 or only a bit more than half the earnings of the average pathologist on percentage of revenue arrangements as revealed in the HCFA survey.

It should be clear by now how much more the hospital-based physicians benefit in personal income by the percentage of revenue arrangements, but one more example from this 1975 study should help even the most skeptical reader to appreciate this situation. The HCFA study further broke down its data into the four regions of the country and found that pathologists on the West Coast averaged twice the incomes of their counterparts on the East Coast ($141,600 and $71,300 respectively).

When the surveyors then compared pathologist compensation practices for the West Coast with the East Coast, the explanation for this remarkable discrepancy immediately became apparent: 91 percent of pathologists on the West Coast operate with percentage of revenue contracts while only 28 percent of pathologists on the East Coast have this arrangement. The same general pattern also was noted for radiologists. A good hospital negotiator will capitalize on this geographical/compensation method discrepancy. Obviously, some very well qualified specialists on the East Coast might be enticed to higher paying salaried positions in the midwest or far west and the availability of such specialists should enhance the hospital's bargaining position dramatically.

Unfortunately, this HCFA study, which was done by Arthur Andersen and Company and Inter Study, Inc., was not able to evaluate the annual earnings of pathologists, radiologists and other hospital-based physicians who billed patients directly on a fee-for-service basis because, short of an I.R.S. audit, this information was not available to the hospitals and such information obviously would not be offered voluntarily by the individual physicians. We can only guess how high these incomes might be. The study does suggest, however, that fee-for-service separate billing can, in fact, be significantly more lucrative than even the percentage of revenue arrangements and this was the most easily detected in the case of anesthesiologists. For instance, even though 68 percent of East Coast anesthesiologists used percentage of revenue arrangements, their average income was only $77,000 compared with $168,000 for West Coast anesthesiologists who almost exclusively used the fee-for-service separate billing plan.

The HCFA study also reveals a steady trend toward fee-for-service billing by radiologists, and within this particular compensation method a very dramatic increase in direct billing and collection of fees by the radiologist. A 1965 study showed that direct billing by radiologists was used by only 7.4 percent, while 10 years later in this HCFA Study, direct billing by radiologists had risen to 28.4 percent.

This important 1977 HCFA study will be referred to again, but I have one final observation of interest at this point. The report from the Wage and Price Council revealed significantly lower median incomes for all physicians in private practice in 1976 as compared with the HCFA data for hospital-based physicians. In 1974 and 1976 (the only two study years available) the median income for all self-employed physicians was $54,140 and $62,799 respectively, compared with the average 1975 incomes of hospital-based radiologists of $103,200, hospital pathologists of $98,400 and anesthesiologists of $80,000. This dramatic difference has potentially great significance in the hospital's contract negotiation process because it can be expected that other physicians such as surgeons, family practitioners and pediatricians may be less inclined to offer backing and political support to these hospital-based physicians in their efforts to negotiate or renegotiate compensation arrangements that will allow them to earn incomes almost twice that of the private-practice physician.

Examples of what real savings can be derived by a hospital (and the public it serves) when percentage of revenue arrangements are eliminated are shown in Figure 1, page 18.

There are obviously significant savings to be found through the elimination of open ended contracts. In fact, Dr. Sidney Wolfe's estimate of $215 million annually in excess costs resulting from these types of contracts with radiologists and pathologists alone may be very conservative, because his estimate is based on only what appears to be the aggregate of excessive personal incomes, and does not take account of potentially unnecessary hospital-based physician over-staffing — as for example when only two pathologists may be required for a particular hospital's laboratory, but four pathologists are supported by the professional income generated by the department.

By the Joint Commission on Accreditation of Hospitals standards, at least one pathologist is considered necessary for the laboratory, but no standards exist for the appropriate number required over and above this. Several instances are known where the chief pathologist employed additional pathologists in his department, even when they were not necessary, simply to anticipate and avoid criticism by the administration that excessive personal incomes were being earned under the percentage arrangement. In the College of American Pathologists' "Manual of Ethical and Contractual Relations" little mention is made of productivity of pathologists under the percentage of revenue contracts. In fact, in a unique stroke of economic logic the "Manual" advises that whenever the income generated on a percentage of revenue basis for the professional practice of pathology . . . "is excessively large, it indicates either the need for the services of an additional pathologist in the depart-

HOSPITAL-BASED PHYSICIAN CONTRACT SAVINGS – CASE EXAMPLE

FIGURE I

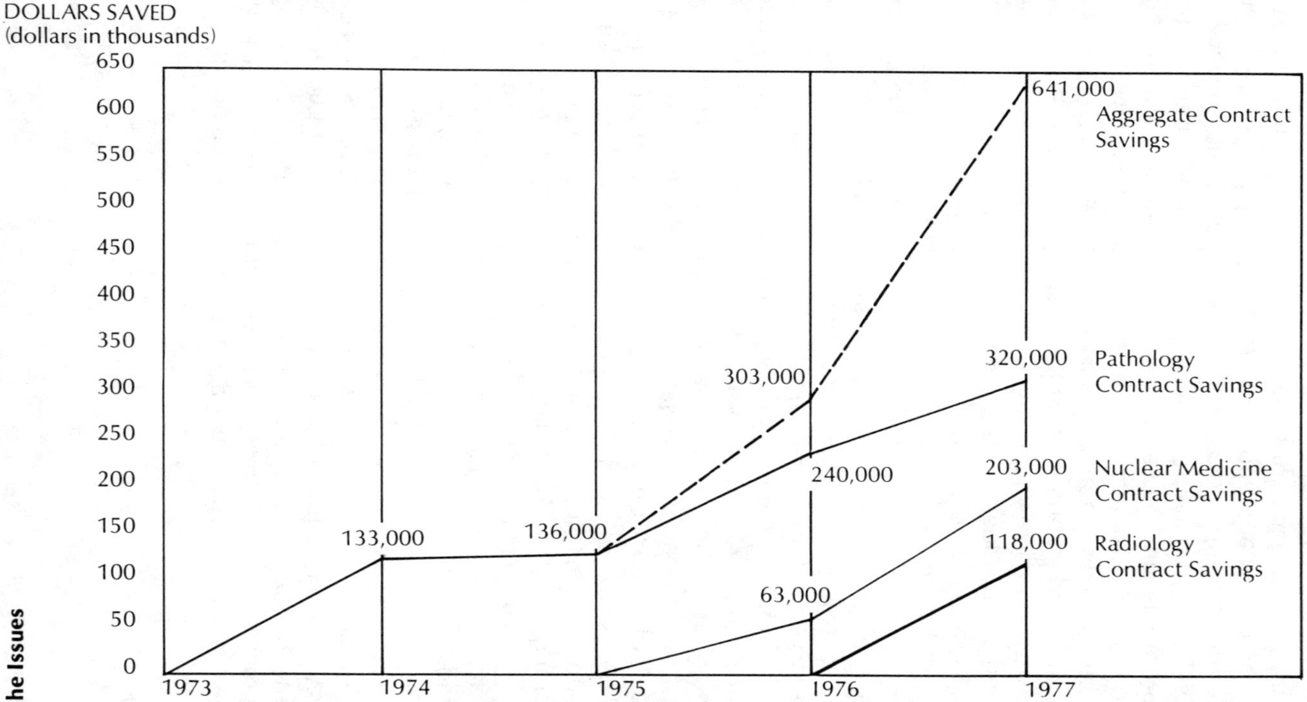

NOTE: 1974 Pathology Contract renegotiated from 25% of gross to straight salaries; 1975 Nuclear Medicine Contract renegotiated from 33% of gross to straight salaries; 1976 Radiology Contract renegotiated from 33% of gross to combined billing by hospital.

NOTE: See Case Examples cited in Chapter VII for two of these contracts.

ment. . .or that fees charged for the pathology services are excessive."

The College in effect leaves it to each pathologist to determine what constitutes an excessive income.

On the matter of professional productivity and compensation, the situation with radiologists and other hospital-based physicians is only slightly less ambiguous, because usually their professional efforts relate in one way or another more directly to the output of their department. Thus the American College of Radiology used to recommend to its membership that approximately 14,000 diagnostic x-ray readings could be considered a reasonable volume for a full-time radiologist to perform annually.

In two Chicago area surveys initiated in 1974 and 1975, the average diagnostic x-ray readings per full-time equivalent radiologist was almost 30 percent higher than this recommended figure. It can be assumed, therefore, that either the productivity standards set by the ACR are unrealistically low or that a great many hospital radiologists in the Chicago area are putting in 12 to 16 hour days.

In preparing for contract negotiations it is important that other implications of this situation not be underestimated or inadequately accounted for. Whenever a contract is negotiated that rewards a hospital-based physician on the basis of the volume of output of his department (whether the arrangement is percentage or fee-for-service), several important conditions need to be considered. On one hand, the professional societies may develop arbitrary ratios of the number of specialists required for a given number of procedures, but then remain silent on the more critical issue of how many specialists are too few for the department's volume of output. The hospital administrator, on the other hand, has to be concerned that he is not sanctioning the employment of more specialists than are needed by the department and also not allowing too few specialists to carry a bigger load than they should — for their own personal gain.

Obviously, three emergency care physicians or three radiologists carrying a workload that normally required four individuals will enhance their income because they don't have to share this with a fourth partner, but they may also compromise the quality of services rendered. For this reason the American Hospital Association's *Guidelines on Contractual Relationships Between Hospitals and Physicians* wisely warns that "As the volume of work increases and additional personnel become necessary, understandably the physician may be reluctant to accept the reduction in his personal income necessary to provide compensation for an additional colleague. Thus . . . a busy department may be permitted to continue understaffed with professional personnel, to the detriment of patient care, unless the safeguard of annual review is carefully adhered to." The annual review referred to here is obviously a review by the administration of the physician staffing in relation to the increasing volume, since it is difficult to review the quality of the department's output *per se*.

Thus far it appears that the financial consequences of these types of contractual arrangements are very dramatic, so much so that we should not be surprised that they have caught the consumer's eye. However, this is only part of the story and the even more complex economic implications have not yet been grasped by the public and the media. In essence, most hospital-based physicians' contracts, notably the percentage of revenue and direct billing arrangements, appear to have been developed with total disregard for the basic laws of economics that apply to most free enterprise industries.

These contracts, it can be argued, create disincentives for productivity and efficiency and encourage excessive utilization of services and constant price escalation.

3. Economic Implications

Trying to understand the Wonderland economics of the hospital industry, and, more specifically, the rules and logic behind these hospital-based physician contracts is likely to be confusing and frustrating. A good sense of humor may be required to get through this section.

The problem starts with a monopoly, a concept that most of us find repugnant and contrary to the basic principles of a free enterprise economy. But it also involves some other strange phenomena including "price inelasticity of demand," "equilibrium pricing," "monopsonies" and situations in which the consumer is not the purchaser (and *vice versa*) and where monopolists subcontract out additional monopolies. Here is a brief summary of some of the fundamentals of the curious economics of the hospital industry and these contractual arrangements which may be useful even if they sound unreal.

First let us look at monopolies. In effect the hospitalized patient is the victim of a whole series of monopolistic practices. If the patient's physician only has admitting privileges at one hospital, the patient basically has no option regarding the hospital in which he will be treated. Once admitted, the patient becomes a captive client. He (or she) has in effect little choice of which diagnostic services will be ordered or by whom it will be provided, no choice of which anesthesiologist will render him unconscious, which radiologist will interpret his x-rays, or even what specialist consultant his physician may call into the case.

Thus, the attending physician controls the demand curve and the patient is the passive, captive consumer of these services. Since the patient basically has had no choice all along the line, he is obviously not in a position to be discriminating as to price; he (or his insurance premiums) has to bear the cost of whatever a specialist consultant or radiologist or pathologist charges for services. The patient's physician is in no position to act as a fiduciary broker or agent for the patient because he, too, has virtually no control over the charges of other physicians, whether they are consultants or hospital-based physicians, and usually the ultimate cost is borne by a remote third party anyway — Medicare, Medicaid, the patient's employer, or insurance, or union.

If you, the consumer, were unhappy with the services of a local restaurant, you could simply refuse to pay for the services or not patronize this restaurant again, and in time if enough customers had the same experiences, the restaurant would close. Or if the restaurant was run inefficiently and the owner had to keep raising his prices to cover his losses, at some point you and other customers would simply not go to the restaurant any longer. In the case of the hospital it is quite different. It is sort of like having a friend (the physician) decide at which restaurant you will eat and what you will order, and then having another friend (government and/or private health insurance companies) pick up the tab for the meal. But even these benevolent people who pick up the tab aren't the ultimate payers of the service; they are intermediaries. The real payers are your company or union if they underwrite your health insurance premiums, or you if you have to pay out of pocket for services, or you again through your Social Security contributions to underwrite government sponsored programs (e.g. Medicare).

Things get even more complicated when the monopolist, the hospital, subcontracts out a special franchise or mini-monopoly to its hospital-based physicians. Such physicians are given an exclusive right to provide services (radiology, pathology, emergency care, etc.) in the hospital; no other radiologists or pathologists are allowed to provide these services once the contract is made. These physicians thus have full control over the supply (and quality) of these services, and the hospitalized patient and his attending physician are fully dependent on this subcontractor, and whatever professional fee he chooses to charge.

Obviously, neither the hospitalized patient nor the attending physician has total freedom to make substitutions once the patient is hospitalized. A seriously ill patient cannot be transferred to another hospital for less costly diagnostic testing, nor can the attending physician send out work to a private laboratory for a hospitalized patient. The hospital-based physician is guaranteed a supply of patients and this is independent of his professional charges for services. That is, if he reduces his professional fees he won't receive any more inpatient referrals, while if he increases his fees he probably won't receive any fewer inpatient referrals.

In economic theory, this phenomenon is called "price inelasticity of demand" and may occur independently of a monopolistic situation. It occurs because the attending physician needs the diagnostic results regardless of what they will cost his patient as well as for several other reasons including the fact that he may not be willing to or capable of making price conscious decisions or that he may have a defensive-medicine motivation to order the tests. In any case, what it means is that hospital-based physicians usually face inelastic price curves because the demand for their services do not vary with price changes.

As the economist Richard Leftwich points out: "The businessman contemplating changes in price of his product should be vitally concerned with its elasticity of demand for the price change. If demand were inelastic a price increase would be advisable but a price decrease would not." The hospital-based physician thus would not benefit in his profits by decreasing his professional fees.

In this unique monopolistic situation with an inelastic price curve no equilibrium price is ever reached, that is, a price that balances demand against supply. Under normal competitive circumstances a low priced service will gradually be driven up to its equilibrium price level because consumers will purchase more of the service at a lower price — up to the point that supply of the service becomes scarce and then the supplier can begin charging higher prices. Under normal circumstances a price above equilibrium will usually cause a surplus (consumers don't buy it) and the supplier has to lower his prices to induce consumers to buy. In either case, equilibrium pricing results. This basically does not work in the case of hospital-based physicians for the reasons cited and, as a consequence, an external body (either the hospital itself or regulatory agencies) has to ensure that a maximum price or fee is set below the monopoly fee so something close to a normal equilibrium price/fee will be obtained.

The foregoing situation is modified when hospital-based physicians are not totally dependent on inpatient referrals, as for example, the hospital radiologists whose department receives 50 percent or more of its caseload from outpatient referrals. In this case, the radiologist has an incentive to keep his professional fees low, to induce more office physicians to refer cases to him. However, third-party reimbursers, namely Blue Cross and Medicare, do not sanction price discrimination for the same services, such as a lower charge for a chest x-ray performed on an outpatient and a higher charge for an inpatient. Thus, the radiologist may want to be price competitive for a portion of his referrals, but doesn't need to be for the inpatient referrals and since price discrimination is not possible he will favor the higher fee structure.

Although it should be fairly easy to understand how this operates with pathologists, radiologists, EKG-EEG-pulmonary function interpreters and other specialists, one might expect emergency care physicians to be unable to take advantage of their monopolistic situation because their services are not provided to captive inpatients. That is, if they charge too much for their professional fees, the consumers may go to another hospital emergency room.

As a matter of fact, emergency physicians are frequently encouraged by their fellow staff physicians to keep their professional charges high — at least higher than the fees primary care physicians (family practitioners, internists, pediatricians and obstetricians) charge for routine office visits, lest their patients begin turning to the hospital's emergency room for routine primary care services. And the true serious emergency patient is more likely to be motivated by geographical proximity than emergency room professional charges in his selection of where to go for services. Thus, the monopoly arrangement benefits even the hospital-based emergency care physician.

In economic theory, this oversimplification demonstrates the importance of the contract negotiation process and the special importance of the hospital's retaining the ultimate authority to regulate professional fees of hospital-based physicians and not allowing open ended contracts.

The courts have typically been supportive of the hospital's right to sanction these special monopolistic arrangements, but most such judicial rulings have been in the relatively clear-cut cases of radiology, pathology, nuclear medicine and other such areas in which major capital and manpower commitments are made by the hospital that require some degree of restrictive access and control by a selected group of medical specialists.

Some cases that upheld the right of the hospital to engage in such contracts include Adler *v.* Montefiore Hospital Association of Western Pennsylvania in 1973 (involving a cardiologist and a hospital cardiac catheterization laboratory), Blank *v.* Palo Alto-Stanford Hospital Center in 1965 (involving radiologists) and Datillo *v.* Tucson General Hospital.

In this third case the administrator's logic for an exclusive contract for a nuclear physician included the fact that such contracts allow control and standardization of departmental procedures and greater consistency of care and also allow the board of trustees to monitor the department and ensure that standards are maintained because of the limited number of physicians involved in the department. This administrator may have been a bit carried away, however, when he went on to say that such exclusive contracts allow the department to operate more economically. Otherwise, he was probably correct and the court so ruled in the hospital's favor.

Governing boards and administrators, however, should be careful not to assume that these exclusive arrangements are beyond challenge or that they can automatically be extended to several new emerging subspecialties or other areas that were formerly open services. For example, this principle might be challenged by a new staff nephrologist who believes he has a right to admit his patients to the hospital-based renal dialysis unit, which heretofore had been under the exclusive medical supervision and clinical management of another group of nephrologists.

If and when a challenge of these monopolistic arrangements ever occurs, there are two legal bases on which it may rest: first, that such contracts may be in violation of state or federal antitrust statutes as a restraint of trade, and second, that it may be an unlawful or unjustified interference in the right to pursue a business or trade. In an interesting legal variation, a Florida radiologist in the Rush *v.* City of St. Petersburg case (1967) used a different tack — and lost. His challenge was based on the same grounds that through such a contract with another group of radiologists the hospital was presumably engaging in the illegal corporate practice of medicine. The suit was not entertained because the radiologist could show no damage to the public through such an arrangement.

Even though these exclusive contracts are probably necessary for the hospital and they have been sanctioned in the courts, their economic implications should not be taken lightly.

Let us look at some of the actual problems and compounding of errors inherent in the specific situation of pathology contracts based on percentage of gross revenue. It does not take a professor of economics to appreciate the inequity and counter-usefulness of this type of contract and yet it still reigns as the one most often specified by pathologists in this country.

First, the percentage of gross income arrangement is monopolistic and not subject to competitive bidding or competition from outside pathologists, resulting in all the potentially negative consequences just discussed.

Second, the pathologist has no incentive to prevent or discourage overutilization of laboratory services by the hospital's medical staff. Why should a pathologist advise a staff physician that a specific series of requested tests is not germane to the diagnosis, if this will result in lost revenue? It is interesting to note, as a corollary, just how few pathologists in this country have embraced the concept of "clinically relevant microbiology," which is basically an exception-reporting approach that stresses identifying only those few organisms that are clinically relevant rather than exhaustive reporting of all organisms. Pathologists have had so little economic incentive to eliminate popular but clinically obsolete tests or procedures that could be performed more efficiently and with more reliable results in other ways that several Blue Cross/Blue Shield Plans had to step in and ban reimbursement for a whole list of such diagnostic tests in 1978.

Third, under the percentage of gross arrangement, whenever the hospital administration is obliged to increase its charges to cover increased laboratory capital and operating costs (resulting from inflationary increases in supply costs and payroll expenses), the pathologists automatically benefit from these increased charges because the department's gross revenues increase.

Fourth, the percentage of gross contracts offers no incentives for efficiency in the management of the laboratory. In fact, laboratory inefficiencies will ultimately result in the hospital's having to increase its laboratory charges to cover these costs and the pathologist thereby becomes the beneficiary of his own department's inefficiencies by sharing in increased gross revenues that result from the increased charges. This was confirmed by the HEW Health Care Financing Administration study referred to earlier. In a complex multivariate analysis of their raw data, HEW showed that hospital-based physicians who work under salary arrangements were less likely than those under percentage of revenue contracts to benefit automatically by increased operating costs of their departments.

Many hospital administrators have recognized this inherent counter-incentive to efficiency in the percentage of gross arrangements and have attempted to offset it by employing laboratory managers or administrative assistants for laboratory service who typically are accountable to an administrative officer for ensuring operational efficiencies in the laboratory. One dramatic example of this can be seen in the reluctance of some chief pathologists to introduce cost efficient automated equipment because the savings that are derived will benefit the hospital (or the public) in the form of reduced charges, or at least a slowing down of charge increases in upcoming years. This, in turn, eventually means less rapid escalation of gross revenues and hence the pathologists' compensation. Similarly, the chief pathologist may be willing to provide a wide range of esoteric procedures which are not cost beneficial for the institution to provide; that is, the department's gross revenues increase even though this may be more than offset in capital and operating costs to the hospital.

Fifth, as almost every hospital administrator knows, private reference laboratories can perform most procedures at significantly less cost than the hospital laboratory can, and yet the pathologist on a percentage of gross arrangement lets contracts for very few reference services — perhaps because he cannot request his normal percentage of gross on procedures that are performed elsewhere.

Sixth, such contracts assure the pathologists no risks and no overhead such as other physicians must face and yet the contract percentage is initially set so the pathologist's compensation is competitive with his free-market counterpart in private practice. The hospital guarantees the pathologist a supply of patients, the technical and clerical manpower to render the services, and the equipment and facilities to do this conveniently, safely and efficiently.

Seventh and last, there is virtually no relation between the number of routine laboratory procedures a hospital laboratory turns out in a year's time and the amount of time, effort and skills the pathologist has to provide. The exception to this, of course, is in the area of surgical pathologic procedures, autopsies and a limited number of other services where the pathologist's time, effort and skills do directly relate to the output. Early in 1970, the Senate Anti-Trust and Monopoly Committee looked at this very issue when it was investigating the whole subject of rising hospital costs and some of the testimony given before that committee is worth quoting:

Dr. John Taylor, President of the Southern Illinois Hospital Corporation: "The pathologist . . . does not order the tests done in the laboratory, he does not perform the tests, and he does not interpret the results or record them. . .the only possible justification for this income from the laboratory is the pathologist's responsibility for the standard of work done there. This admittedly is quite important, but could be achieved by a well qualified technician supervisor who runs the laboratory."

Dr. Taylor pointed out that less than 10 percent of the laboratory revenues generated by hospitals in his corporation related to actual pathology. . .the other ninety percent relating to chemistry and other traditional testing. Relative to tissue and organ examinations and autopsies, Dr. Taylor added: "This is the real value of a pathologist and good medical practice absolutely depends on this for quality care. . .this cannot be done by anyone else."

Also, during these 1970 Senate hearings, Roma Brown, then president of the American Society of Medical Technologists, said "Most of the tests are performed by technologists and reported directly to the attending physician without any direct activity by the pathologist. . .and the vast majority of lab results are utilized by the attending physician without consultation with the pathologist." A footnote: Miss Brown was dismissed from her job as laboratory manager at her hospital when she returned from giving her Senate testimony.

Incidentally, even though the percentage-of-revenue pathologists will strongly argue that their supervision and quality control monitoring of the performance of the technicians is an awesome responsibility, I know of no judicial decision that has ever found the pathologists liable for the errors of a hospital laboratory technician, and the hospital, as the employer, is fully responsible for absorbing the risk of negligence of its technical staff.

This point about the limited involvement of the pathologist in the actual output of his department separates the pathologists from other hospital-based physicians, and has been a very sensitive issue with the College of American Pathologists. It was the C.A.P., more than any other professional society, that mobilized all its lobbying efforts to prevent a stipulation in the Medicare Act that would allow Part B (medical services as opposed the Part A, hospital services) reimbursement only for "identifiable service requiring performance by a physician in person."

If this stipulation had remained in the Act, pathologists would have been forced to confess that they are personally and directly involved in only about 10 percent of the output of their departments, which would have been reimbursable under Part B. Consequently this meant their remaining 90 percent of compensation would have to come under the Part A portion, which would clearly define their role as 90 percent supervisory. The next logical question that would have been asked by administrators and boards of trustees is: Should the hospital continue to pay $100,000 or more annually for simple supervisory functions alone? (Generally, the Social Security Administration reached a compromise whereby reimbursement could be provided on either basis — Part A or Part B and thereby did not precipitate this issue.)

Although the foregoing seven strange and counter-economic principles raised here underlie the percentage of gross arrangement with pathologists, they also apply equally well to radiologists and other hospital-based specialists in these arrangements. Similar deficiencies apply to other percentage of revenue contracts whether they are percentage of gross with an upper limit, or with a sliding scale, or percentage of net income. The main problem with percentage of net arrangements is trying to determine what "net" really means and this in itself becomes a negotiating nightmare.

It might be interesting to know how revenue sharing contracts developed in the first place so perhaps we can understand why, in defiance of all logic, they continue to persist; also it might help us anticipate how the new direct billing approval will be "sold" to hospitals.

One of the most basic problems is that there has traditionally been an undersupply of these physicians, and theirs' has been a seller's market. The fields of pathology and radiology have lacked the glamour and prestige of other medical specialties. In 1971, for example, only 69 percent of all available pathology residencies were filled (compared with an 85 percent fill rate for all medical specialty residencies), and the majority

(55 percent) of these pathology residencies were filled by foreign medical graduates.

Also even though pathologists are directly involved in about only 10 percent of laboratory procedures, the Joint Commission on Accreditation of Hospitals standards require a pathologist-director of the laboratory and the J.C.A.H. requires that all x-rays taken in hospitals be interpreted by radiologists. Therefore, at least as it applies to pathologists and radiologists, owing to tight supply conditions plus the J.C.A.H. standards, these physicians have been in relatively strong bargaining positions, and could demand favorable contract terms from hospitals.

More important than this is the inherently confused status of the relationship between these physicians and the patient. If they were specialists who were called in on consultation by attending physicians, they could bill the patient for a consultant's fee. But the simple reading and interpretation of x-ray films (which does not constitute a final diagnosis) or the evaluation and interpretation of tissue abnormalities and the supervision of technical staff in providing laboratory results, raise questions about these types of activity as true consultations. In 1957 the J.C.A.H. unequivocally precluded consultation billing by these specialists for such services: "Under no circumstances does the Joint Commission believe that x-ray examinations, electrocardiogram determinations or pathological tissue examinations constitute consultations in our sense of the word."

Because physicians traditionally have an aversion to salaries, apparently some other option had to be found and since the chief pathologist and chief radiologist were usually aware of the gross income generated from their departments, no doubt they found their salaries paltry by comparison, especially in view of the fact that they may have resented what appeared to be the hospital's making huge profits from their medical skills —an obvious violation of the old medical taboo against the corporate practice of medicine.

There is no question that administrators did, and still do, encourage excessively high net incomes from such ancillary departments to help underwrite high loss areas elsewhere in the hospital. This practice is a remnant of a period prior to Medicare and other third-party reimbursement and major medical coverage insurance; when most patients paid part or all of the cost of care hospital charges were not allocated in relation to cost, and high profit margins did accrue to these ancillary departments.

To get a share of these profits hospital radiologists and pathologists contrived a uniquely obscure formula but it was so confusing for administrators that it was beyond comprehension and challenge. In the 1961 American College of Radiologists' "Guide for Radiologists in Relationship with Institutions," the following logic is offered for a 35 to 45 percent percentage of gross arrangements:

"Extensive data in the college files discloses the fact that x-ray department costs, both direct and indirect, plus allowance for amortization, depreciation and reasonable return on investment do not exceed 50 percent of gross collections in the average private general hospital. [Therefore] the radiologists should retain 40 percent (plus or minus 5 percent) of gross billings, contracts based on retention of less than 35 percent are regarded as improper."

The College of American Pathologists was not to be outdone, and its reasoning is expressed in the Manual of Ethical and Contractual Relationships as follows:

"Budget items based on gross charges which include 20 percent for concession in lieu of rent and minor utilities, 30-40 percent for supplies, equipment and non-physician personnel, 2 percent for bookkeeping and 10 percent for uncollectible debts.

"These amounts of gross charges make up the total of operational expenses of the department. The remaining amount is the income for the professional practice of pathology."

An alert administration would quickly figure that this latter formula means the pathologist is entitled to 28 to 38 percent of the gross charges of his department.

Almost 20 years later these suggested percentages remain close to the current figures used in most hospitals that employ percentage of gross contracts, namely about 25 percent for pathology and 35 percent for radiology. Therefore, what these Colleges' formulas lack in the way of economic logic, they apparently make up for in economic foresight. Such contracts — and even these specific percentages — are apparently still acceptable to the majority of hospitals in this country in spite of the major financial impacts of Medicare, Medicaid, rate review commissions, rapid increases in personnel costs, F.I.C.A., Workmen's Compensation, Unemployment Compensation, exponential increases in hospital liability/malpractice insurance premiums and energy and thus utility costs, and a costly technological explosion in these ancillary departments.

Because of the Medicare retroactive adjustment factor, administrators who have not revised their original percentage of gross arrangements, have let this cost-related loss fall on the hospital alone.

Under these circumstances, to keep from going into the red the hospital administrator now is forced to continue escalating his ancillary charges to compensate for the widening gap in third-party cost reimbursement arrangements, inflationary factors, new costs associated with regulatory processes such as ERISA, OSHA, etc., and the costs of staying current with technological advances. His ancillary charge structure will get farther and farther away from a cost related base, and more unbearable to patients who are not fully covered by health insurance.

These percentage of revenue arrangements were also the natural consequence of the efforts of the professional societies to ban or otherwise discourage their members from accepting salaried positions. The Justice Department has not been totally silent or naive on these antitrust and restraint of trade efforts. In a Justice Department suit against the College of American Pathologists initiated in 1966, a consent decree was finally handed down in 1969 that prohibited any coercion or related action against its members (and its affiliated members, Registered Medical Technologists) who accept salaried employment.

In 1966, expressing its dissatisfaction with several reimbursement provisions of the Medicare Act, the American College of Radiology announced that it was closing its placement bureau to hospitals that would not allow a direct billing option for their radiologists. As of 1973 a similar action was apparently still in use by the C.A.P. to make its placement listings unavailable to hospitals, and restricted these only to chief pathologists of the hospital, thereby making it very difficult for a hospital to recruit a replacement for a chief pathologist who refused to accept a salary or some similar arrangement.

As recently as 1978 a Federal Trade Commission consent order required the American Society of Anesthesiologists to withdraw its opposition to hospital employment for its members, and to delete from its files any past records of censure against individual members for not complying with A.S.A.'s previous position.

4. Impact of Cost Reimbursement and Regulated Rate Setting

In the 1977 HEW-sponsored *Study of Reimbursement and Practice Arrangements of Provider Based Physicians* that was cited earlier, the Health Care Financing Administration surveyors tried to determine if the way a hospital was reimbursed (*i.e.*, relatively higher charge-related reimbursement *vs.* cost-related reimbursement) affected the types of hospital-based physician compensation agreements the hospital used, and what financial effects, if any, this had for the hospital.

The results confirmed the surveyors' hypothesis that hospitals with relatively low cost reimbursements tended to favor salaried contracts with their radiologists and pathologists, and the incomes earned by hospital-based physicians in these hospitals were therefore significantly lower than the incomes earned in the other hospitals with high cost-related reimbursement — which also had relatively higher proportions of hospital-based physicians on percentage of revenue arrangements.

For example, in those hospitals that derived more than 50 percent of their revenues from cost based reimbursements, only 15 percent of their radiologists were on salary and 57 percent were on percentage of revenue arrangements. The average earnings of radiologists in these hospitals was $113,100 compared with only $80,600 for radiologists in hospitals that were less than 50 percent cost reimbursed (where more radiologists worked on salary in contrast to percentage of revenue arrangements). Similar results were noted with the pathologists. What this appears to mean is that hospital administrators have a greater incentive to negotiate the more efficient salary contracts when most of these contract savings will enhance the hospital's net income. When the hospital is largely cost reimbursed, the hospital has less incentive to negotiate low cost contracts (salaries) and are more inclined to allow percentage of revenue arrangements to persist.

This exposes one of the fundamental problems with the current cost containment thrust in hospitals throughout the country, especially as it applies to cost containment in hospital-based contracts. For example, if a hospital receives 80 percent of its revenues from cost-reimbursing third parties and it somehow renegotiates a $500,000 pathologist group's contract down to, say, $200,000, this does not represent $300,000 net gain to the hospital. Rather, the value of this successful negotiation is only $60,000, *i.e.* 20 percent of charge reimbursed revenues *times* the $300,000 contract savings. But if on the other hand the hospital's over-all revenues were only 30 percent cost reimbursed (as is probably the case in most nonurban community hospitals), the same example of the successful contract renegotiation from $500,000 down to $200,000, would under this situation add $210,000 to the hospital's net income, *i.e.* 70 percent charge reimbursement *times* the $300,000 contract reduction.

Now if we take this latter example one step farther and add a new assumption: that instead of letting this $210,000 real savings simply improve the hospital's net income, the board of trustees decided to plow it directly back to the public by reducing all laboratory charges by an amount equivalent to $210,000. If the pathologists were still on a percentage of revenue contract, though now reduced in percentage by the contract renegotiation to yield only $200,000 income, it is obvious that the board's proposed reduction in laboratory charges would further reduce the pathologists' projected earnings because their earnings are based on the percentage of laboratory charges or income generated. Clearly, the pathologists would not take kindly to the board's directive to reduce laboratory charges under these circumstances, whereas if the pathologists were now on salary it would not make any difference to them how the board chose to distribute this savings — either as an increase in the institution's net operating income to underwrite other departments or as a reduction in laboratory charges. This dilemma will undoubtedly raise some interesting challenges for state rate review commissions as they begin to face the harsh economic reality of percentage of revenue arrangements followed in most hospitals.

The HCFA study does give us some insight into how prospective rate setting commissions may have an impact on the whole issue of hospital-based physicians and their compensation arrangements. Unfortunately, the data can at best only be suggestive because there are still only 10 state legislatures that have created rate review mechanisms. As might be suspected, the HCFA results suggest that prospective rate setting may have a downward impact on the earnings of hospital-based physicians if applied to their specialty departments.

As occurred in the embattled implementation of the 1965 Medicare Act, we can expect the hospital-based physician once again to be planted, by choice or as pawn, on a battle line to test how far state rate review commissions can go before all physicians' fees come under regulation. In May 1978, Maryland's Montgomery County Circuit Court ruled in favor of the Maryland Health Service Cost Review Commission in its efforts to regulate charges of hospital-based radiologists, pathologists and other specialists, no matter what their contracts allowed, whether they bill separately or as a percentage of gross revenues, or whether they classify themselves as independent contractors or hospital employees. This was a very significant decision.

The Maryland Commission took the position that in-hospital services performed by pathologists, radiologists and cardiologists were hospital services and therefore within its jurisdiction as a rate review agency. The Circuit Court's supportive ruling was apparently based on the fact that no traditional patient-physician relationship is involved and hospital-based physicians provide services that are ancillary to those of other physicians.

Maryland's Court of Appeals ultimately overruled the Circuit Court decision and thereby decided that the state's rate review commission had not been empowered to regulate the fees of these hospital-based specialists. The Court of Appeals did, however, return the suit to the Circuit Court to decide whether the commission's authority as it relates to the so-called "cost of the hospital" embraced the cost of hospital-based physicians. It is conceivable that should rate review commissions ultimately obtain this authority, but be unable to extend the rate review authority to hospital-based physicians who bill directly or to those who lease facilities from the hospital, a renewed effort toward adoption of these types of contracts may become evident.

What administrators should anticipate in any case is that there will be a definite effort by pathologists and radiologists to get out of the percentage of revenue arrangements in states that have, or will have, rate review commissions. Whatever the result of the Maryland test case relative to the hospital-based physician component, per se, tough rate setting could be applied to laboratory and x-ray charges and thereby indirectly reduce the earnings of these revenue sharing pathologists and radiologists. Along these lines, George Tyler, attorney for the Maryland State Pathology Association, warned that even if the commission loses "it'll probably continue to issue aggregate orders addressing total costs, letting hospitals and pathologists fight it out among themselves to decide who gets what."

5. Medicare Impact

Of all the issues surrounding the problem of hospital-based physician contracts, the implementation of the Medicare Act is unquestionably the most bloated pseudo-issue to surface, and even now, more than a decade later, we can still hear well intentioned attorneys, C.P.A. consultants, hospital administrators and, of course, hospital-based physicians talking about the importance of Part A and Part B., deductibles and co-insurance provisions, "reasonable charge" provisions, etc., as critical considerations in developing or renegotiating hospital-based physician contracts.

The Medicare impact is really of practical value in only two respects. First, not unlike the current rate review commission's efforts, it is giving the various professional societies a basis on which to urge their members to move toward fee-for-service direct billing — and this will become a serious negotiation problem for many hospitals. Second, the conflicts and reactions of hospital-based physicians *vis-a-vis* the proposed compensation methods exposed some of the serious professional insecurities of hospital-based physicians.

Without a doubt the hospital-based physician compensation provisions in the Medicare Act turned out to be one of the most controversial aspects of the Medicare legislation. But as Somers and Somers point out in their excellent book *Medicare and the Hospitals — Issues and Perspectives,* "Medicare did not create the 'specialist problem,' but it did exacerbate previous difficulties and added some disruptive influences of its own."

As has been noted there has been a definite trend toward more fee-for-service direct billing arrangements over the past several years and to a large extent this relates to the implementation of Medicare and the subsequent efforts of some professional societies to seize this as an opportunity to finally get their specialties out from under the control and influence of hospitals.

Based on a report entitled *Hospital-Based Specialists Study: Pathologists' and Radiologists' Arrangements with Hospitals 1965-1968* made by Frank Van Dyke on behalf of the Columbia University School of Public Health and Administrative Medicine, there was a dramatic increase in fee-for-service arrangements by radiologists shortly after the implementation of Medicare in 1965. In that year this relatively uncommon arrangement was used by only 9 percent of radiologists. By 1968 it had soared to the second commonest radiologists' compensation arrangement with 29 percent of radiologists adopting it.

Admittedly, not all of these arrangements were direct billing fee-for-service as distinguished from combined billing fee-for-service; however, the conclusion in the 1977 HCFA study was that "Most of this increase can be attributed to a movement by radiologists to what we have termed 'direct billing'." Somers and Somers also noted that in just 12 months between Dec. 31, 1965, and Dec. 31, 1966, direct billing arrangements by radiologists jumped from 12.5 percent to 30.1 percent while billing of radiologist services by the hospital declined from 88.7 percent in 1965 to 82.1 percent in 1966. A similar but less dramatic trend was noted by Somers and Somers for pathologists, *i.e.* 11.1 percent direct billing arrangements in 1965 *vs.* 17.9 percent in 1966. As one might expect, it is significantly more cumbersome for pathologists to bill patients directly for the several hundred thousand tests a laboratory may perform in a year's time, and this probably explains the restraint shown by pathologists in changing their billing methods.

How did the Medicare Act fuel this move toward direct billing? In its original form, prior to an amendment by the Ways and Means Committee, the King-Anderson Bill would have allowed all hospital contracts with their hospital-based physicians to continue as they had in the past. Following the Committee amendment the law would require all physicians, including hospital-based specialists, to be reimbursed for services to Medicare patients on a "reasonable charge" basis (via Part B — Medical portion) rather than "reasonable cost" basis under Part A, which applied to hospital services.

Sen. Paul Douglas, in a statement to the Senate, succinctly summarized what consequences this revision would have: "What they have done is to begin the bludgeoning of hospitals, which now have agreements with the medical specialists providing for payment through the hospital, into giving up these arrangements. . . .There is little doubt that this use of the federal government to force the hospitals and their medical specialists, who have freely entered into these arrangements, to abandon them was precisely what the A.M.A. and the special group lobbyists actually intended."

As a matter of fact the law did not require changes in existing contracts (at least not toward direct billing) but some extreme editorial liberties were taken by the various medical societies in interpreting the law to mean that "independent" and "separate billing" were now mandatory; separation of professional fees was deliberately misinterpreted so "separate billing" became synonymous with "direct billing." A remarkable campaign by these societies was waged immediately following enactment of this law and many hospital administrators succumbed to the so-called "mandates" to grant direct billing agreements, with the resultant rapid increase in the number of these types of contracts in just 12 months following enactment of the law.

While the American College of Radiology promoted direct billing, the College of American Pathologists tended to favor lease and concession arrangements because of the obvious difficulties in direct billing for laboratory tests. Here are some of the interesting guidelines issued by the ACR Board of Chancellors on October 1, 1965:

"1. Radiologists SHOULD bill patients for their professional services. . .and,

"2. A radiologist should NOT allow the hospital to present a bill for his professional services on or as part of a hospital bill.

"3. A. A radiologist may not ethically pool his professional fees with the hospital service charge.

B. Where the radiologist receives an individual, differentiated fee for his professional medical services, the

> sharing of this fee with hospitals, or other physicians — except in group practice — is clearly fee splitting and unethical."

These directives and admonitions undoubtedly had a sobering effect on many radiologists who until that time probably felt comfortable and ethical in their hospital relationship. This proclamation also must have rattled more than a few hospital administrators and trustees — a very independent position taken by a group which only one year earlier had been viewed as an integral part of hospitals.

Perhaps to declare their final victory in the long battle to win complete independence from hospitals clearly and unambiguously, the November 1965 ACR *Bulletin* further advised its membership that contracts between hospitals and radiologists were no longer really necessary: "The separate billing of the patient for costs by the hospital and for the professional fee by the radiologist eliminates the absolute necessity for a hospital-radiologist agreement." In what was apparently a momentary return to harsh reality, the ACR went on to advise: "Radiologists may meet resistance from hospital administrators in following these recommendations. . .much tact, determination and patience will be required to bring about separate billing by hospitals. However, the obligation of the current physicians to preserve the status of the specialty within medicine makes the effort imperative."

Shortly after the Medicare Act became law, a special Technical Advisory Committee on Specialists' Services was convened to assist the Social Security Administration in implementing the Act so its provisions would not cause a serious inflation of physicians' charges and unnecessary elimination of current contracts that were in compliance with the law. In subsequent guidelines that were issued by the Social Security Administration and the Health Insurance Benefits Advisory Council a relatively simple, though not totally satisfactory, compromise was found. Basically, the compromise allowed hospitals and hospital-based physicians to retain or develop their own contractual relationships and the reimbursement related to Part A versus Part B could be distributed by easily negotiated formulas. In essence, though, it did not require hospital-based physicians to bill directly or independently, as the ACR, CAP and AMA continued to support with their membership, presumably as the original intent of the law, and only those hospital administrators who were not closely following the deliberations of the Social Security Administration, instead of listening to the professional societies, fell prey to their pathologists' and radiologists' demands for direct billing contracts. The American Hospital Association also warned its member hospitals against premature renegotiation of direct billing, fee-for-service contracts with its hospital-based physicians.

The difficulties experienced by hospital-based physicians and hospitals over the Medicare issue did not cease in the 1960's. By 1976 the Health Subcommittee of the Senate Finance Committee was at it again in the Medicare and Medicaid Administrative and Reimbursement Reform Act. During testimony before the Senate subcommittee, Sen. Herman Talmadge was informed that some percentage of revenue contract physicians were earning incomes up to $500,000 annually. Although the proposed revisions were not implemented in 1976, a key clause was proposed. It would have (1) prohibited any percentage of revenue contracts from being eligible for inclusion in Medicare costs and (2) authorized the Secretary of Health, Education and Welfare to determine in advance the reasonableness of all hospital-based physician contracts.

Surprisingly, the American Hospital Association allied itself with the College of American Pathologists, the American Medical Association, the Association of American Medical Colleges and others in opposition to this clause. The A.H.A. stated in its September 1976 *President's Letter* that "On occasion, it seems that a contract may result in excessive compensation, but it is our position that there is not sufficient evidence of abuse to justify the intervention of these proposed revisions." AHA member hospitals were then encouraged "to solve the problem themselves, and AHA's *Guidelines on Contractual Relationships Between Hospitals and Physicians* should be helpful where a problem does exist."

The real significance of the Medicare issue as it pertains to the hospital-based physicians is that hospital-based physicians preferred being included under the Part B provisions of the law for several reasons:

1. It would allow them to be reimbursed on charges rather than costs, and, presumably, with the freedom to establish their own reasonable charges they would stand to gain financially.

2. It would remove them from a dependence on the hospital for reimbursement, and, thereby, offer the prospects of total independence from the institution.

3. It would assure them recognition in the medical community as fellow physicians who like all private practitioners would be grouped under Part B.

6. The Ethics of Medical Economics

Basically, the question this section speaks to is: Are certain hospital-based physician contracts and compensation methods unethical, and if so, should the hospital terminate these arrangements? Like several other deep-seated issues, the heat of the Medicare confrontation caused some so-called medical ethical issues to be exposed and we were able to witness with greater clarity how the medical profession sometimes will attempt to invoke ethics as a defense to economic issues.

At the A.M.A. House of Delegates meeting in June 1966, there was talk of boycott and the introduction of the infamous "Resolution 104" by the Oregon delegation, and subsequently reiterated by the Ohio delegation. Through some strange logic, this position resolved "that since separate (direct) billing by the physician for his professional services is a preferred ethical practice, it shall be deemed unethical for a physician to displace a hospital-based physician who is attempting to practice separate billing when said displacement is primarily designed to circumvent separate (direct) billing." This resolution which passed the A.M.A. house of delegates had the effect of an illegal boycott against hospitals that might choose to negotiate more favorable nondirect billing contracts, and the Justice Department's Anti-Trust Division was quick to advise the A.M.A. what actions might be forthcoming if this resolution remained intact.

The A.M.A. board of trustees ultimately overrode its own house of delegates on this issue and warned its membership:

"Physicians cannot avoid legal consequences of certain actions merely by categorizing them as 'ethical' or 'unethical'. . . . To describe an ethical principle or rule of conduct for physicians does not preclude a court or jury from determining that its purpose is the unreasonable restraint of trade."

This strong, unambiguous statement put an end to the ethical and quasi-legal defense that the delegates had enlisted in the support of direct billing. A different tack was required and the following A.M.A. resolutions indicate the defense was now to be in the area of the staff's prerogatives to ensure quality of patient care (with no use of the word "ethics") and also indirectly a call to non-hospital-based physicians to support the hospital-based physicians:

"If hospital privileges are denied to a physician solely because he chooses to engage in medical practice in accordance with legally acceptable arrangements that are in the best interest of the patients and the medical profession, but unacceptable to the governing board of the hospital, then soon all members of the medical staff can expect a deterioration in the quality of medical care provided to the hospitalized patients and in the conditions under which medicine is practiced within hospitals." The resolutions went further, indicating that "whenever hospital-based physicians and hospitals have contractual differences it is the prerogative and responsibility of the entire medical staff to review the problem. . .investigate and determine the facts and then the hospital-based physician should be supported accordingly by the medical staff."

This veiled threat of having to take on the entire medical staff if a hospital administrator refused to allow a renegotiation of a hospital-based physician arrangement to direct billing was apparently sufficient to discourage many administrators and boards. It is interesting how things have changed since 1966, probably because of the exorbitant compensations some hospital-based physicians have subsequently derived from their special arrangements. In the February 1977 issue of *Hospital Medical Staff,* in an article entitled "Contractual Arrangements Between Physicians and Hospitals — A Physician's View," its author, a pathologist, now seems to be suggesting that hospital-based physicians no longer want medical staff involvement in their contract relationships with the hospital: "The pathologist's compensation should not be a matter for general staff review but should be negotiated by the administration, the board and the candidate. . . .It is true that a pathologist does occupy a sole proprietorship in the hospital laboratory. . .but his professional fee should no more be scrutinized by the medical staff than should that of a surgeon who limits his practice to one institution."

In summary, then, with the ethical issue of these contracts put back in the closet, the professional societies now accepted the fact that as long as they did not transgress the rules established by the government or the courts, they had the legal right to shape their strategies without reference to anything but their membership's personal incomes, professional freedoms, and quality of care issues.

7. Corporate Practice of Medicine Issue

The whole question of whether the hospital is engaging in the corporate practice of medicine in certain of its contractual relationships with physicians was once a critical factor that had to be considered. However, like most other issues, it, too, offered hospital-based physicians more promise than performance and where statutory law once gave it credence, it is now only a vague ethical issue — except in those few states where the anachronistic statute has survived in one form or another.

The original purpose of these state statutes was to ensure that the practice of medicine was restricted to an individual, a licensed medical practitioner, and never a corporate entity — presumably to prevent quackery and the commercialization of the provision of professional medical services. Under this statute it was generally recognized that a hospital, as a corporate entity, could not pay a physician a fixed compensation and bill patients for services rendered by the physician, unrelated to his salary, without being guilty of the illegal practice of medicine as a corporation.

From a practical point of view, the objection was that no corporation should be allowed to profit from the professional services of a physician, and apparently the fear was that hospitals could hire a physician on a salaried basis and then resell his services to patients for a profit. To this day, some hospital-based physicians still will raise the specter of the presumed illegal, unethical corporate practice of medicine and unfair profiteering of hospitals from their efforts.

In the last 80 years many things have occurred that essentially negate all these arguments. Very few states still have these statutes on their books and in those that do there is usually an allowance that nonprofit, charitable corporations may employ physicians at a fixed salary so long as the physicians are not selling their services for a profit. Also, so many expedient exceptions have been introduced into these statutes that those remaining probably have little likelihood of surviving a legal test any longer. Exceptions have been made for public hospitals, university hospitals, and health maintenance organizations, and all state's Workmen Compensation laws allowed salaried industrial physicians in corporations to furnish medical care for their employees.

Again, with the relatively more favorable tax implications to be gained by incorporating (including pension funds, income deferring privileges, fringe benefits), many physicians throughout the United States have chosen to become incorporated, and obviously the statutes had to be modified to take account of this.

In some cases it is certainly questionable whether the many new hospital-based physicians should have the right to profit from the hospital while the hospital is expressly prohibited from profiting from the physicians. A guaranteed minimum compensation to a private, independent contracting emergency physician (a common practice used in virtually all states), may be nothing more than a salaried subsidy of these physicians, at the expense of the hospital and the public when the volume of such patients is not sufficient to cover the cost of this subsidy. Presumably it is also all right if the hospital has to cover the losses related to nonpaying patients or uncollectible accounts, but the emergency physician is not expected to share in any risks of personal income loss.

Also, when a private emergency physician's corporation is established to serve a hospital or a group of hospitals, typically these physicians are salaried and the physician owners of this corporation are thereby making a profit from the services of other physicians. Even in the case where a pathologist is incorporated and hires two associates, the same basic conflict with the corporate practice of medicine concept applies.

Similarly, it would not stretch logic too far to argue that reverse exploitation also takes place when the anesthesiologist uses nurse anesthetists to perform some of their functions under his supervision. In fact, any nurse, technician, intern, resident or paraprofessional whose functions allow the radiologist, pathologist, anesthesiologist or emergency physician to perform their services more efficiently or more expeditiously is in a sense being exploited by these hospital-based physicians — for the physician's profit.

One of the stickiest questions raised by the Medicare conflict about the real medical role of such hospital-based physicians related to a revision in the Medicare Act that would only allow Part B (Medical Services) reimbursement for identifiable services performed by a physician in person. Although after much lobbying by the College of American Pathologists the clause was modified, what was apparently at stake here was the possible exclusion of about 85 to 90 percent of what most pathologists received compensation for (*i.e.* clinical laboratory services) as nonmedical services.

The same basic issues arose again in the proposed 1976 revisions of the Medicare Act under Sen. Herman Talmadge's subcommittee, and also became a major issue in the 1978 effort by Maryland's rate review commission to regulate such hospital-based physicians' charges as a hospital service rather than a strictly medical service.

8. The Independent Contractor and Respondeat Superior Issue

I will not pretend to understand all the ramifications of the law as it relates to the question of hospital-based physicians as so-called independent practitioners. However, there appear to be so many obvious inconsistencies in this whole area that once again like the problem with monopolies, it may not require an expert, a professor of law, to see what is wrong in this situation. Of special relevance is that it not only exposes some deep seated attitudes of physicians relative to their desire for autonomy, but also highlights many of the failures of hospital management and governing boards to make clear their ultimate responsibility for the quality of medical care practiced in their institutions.

On behalf of hospital-based physicians, their attorneys frequently insist on a clause in the contract that defines the physician as an independent contractor, and unfortunately until only recently (with the direct employment of more and more hospital attorneys who understand internal operations of hospitals), the hospital's legal consultants' usually favored these clauses as potential protection for the hospital, should the hospital-based physician be sued for an act of negligence.

The problem with the inclusion of this simple clause is that it deceives both the hospital and the hospital-based physician into believing that the physician is really autonomous. And then both parties begin to act as if this were true — the physician acting as if he is not accountable to anyone but himself and the hospital management acting as if it has no rights or responsibilities in regard to the services (and charges for service) in these areas.

The courts have in the past held otherwise and it is remarkable how few hospital administrators have apparently recognized or accepted the implications of these judicial rulings.

The ultimate absurdity, surprisingly more common in practice than could be imagined, is the situation wherein the hospital administrator, his board and his legal advisers allow an "independent contractor" clause in a salary contract. Under salary contracts the master/servant relationship clearly exists and the doctrine of *Respondeat Superior* must be applicable since the hospital, as the employer, obviously can control the conduct and performance of its employed hospital-based specialist through its ultimate authority to dismiss the employee if he fails to meet performance requirements. In Hodges *v.* Doctors Hospital, a 1977 Georgia case involving an emergency physician, the court made it very clear that even if the hospital does not manifest its control over these physicians, the fact remains that the hospital had the right to do so and the doctrine of *Respondeat Superior* was upheld, the hospital being held responsible for this physician's acts.

More important than this obvious situation is the fact that the courts have found the hospital ultimately responsible, either under the concept of corporate neglect or under *Respondeat Superior,* for ensuring compliance in all aspects of the quality of care rendered in its institution — including medical care. The landmark case was Darling *v.* Charleston Community Memorial Hospital (1965) in Illinois and it is surprising how many hospital trustees have never even heard of this decision, more than a decade after its impact. Although this case which involved negligent acts of an on-call emergency physician, did not speak to the physician's responsibility to the hospital through the doctrine of *Respondeat Superior,* nor did it impose liability on the hospital for the negligence of one of its physicians, it did speak to the hospital's corporate negligence for not ensuring compliance with its standards for the practice of medical care at the institution. Variations of this institutional responsibility were confirmed in several cases in at least seven other states. These cases include Mitchell County Hospital Authority *v.* Joiner (1972, Georgia), Purcell and Tucson General Hospital *v.* Zimbelman (1972, Arizona), Pederson *v.* Dumouchel (1967, Washington) and the infamous Gonzales *v.* Nork case (1973, California) in which in a finding against the hospital itself, the court concluded that "like every governing board, they (the board of this hospital) are corporately responsible for the conduct of their medical staff."

If the governing body of a hospital is responsible to this degree for all of its independent contracting private practitioners, it would certainly be expected that no less responsibility should apply to its relationships with hospital-based physicians, and even if *Respondeat Superior* was not the key issue, a corporate responsibility exists in the contractual arrangements the hospital establishes with its hospital-based physicians.

More typically, *Respondeat Superior* is still the basis in the several cases that found the hospital responsible for its hospital-based physicians, no matter what the compensation arrangements are — salary, direct billing, percentage of revenue, or other. In Beeck *v.* Tucson General Hospital (Arizona, 1972) the hospital was held responsible for the negligence of one of its percentage-of-revenue radiologists. The court applied the doctrine that a master is responsible for a servant's acts in view of the fact that the patient had no choice of a radiologist, as well as the fact that the court viewed this percentage of revenue relationship with the hospital as a contract of employment. The court also rejected an argument based on the distinction between "administrative" and "professional" duties as being confusing and inequitable.

In a more complicated case in Indiana — Keene *v.* Methodist Hospital (1971) — the hospital contended that the radiologist, as a partner of the director of the radiology department, was an independent contractor. The court's response: "The defendant (Methodist Hospital) contends that it is not responsible for the negligence of this radiologist since he is an independent contractor. It is the opinion of the Court that the relationship of this radiologist to the defendant Hospital was much more nearly that of an employee working on a piecework basis, rather than that of a typical independent contractor."

In a 1976 case in New York (Mduba *v.* Benedictine Hospital) the court unequivocally held the hospital responsible for the negligence of an emergency physician irrespective of the type of contract, because the hospital had authority to exercise control over its own emergency room, and, therefore, *Respondeat Superior* was applicable.

In another case involving the emergency department (Snelson *v.* Margaretville Hospital — New York, 1975), the hospital was sued as an employer, even though the emergency physician was a private practitioner on fee-for-service direct billing. Although the hospital was entitled to a summary judgment, the critical issue was that the claimant argued that the hospital should be liable based on the appearance of an employee-employer relationship between this doctor and the hospital, at least as it was perceived by the public.

In the Mehlman *v.* Powell case (Maryland, 1977) the courts finally went the whole way on what the Snelson case had just begun to raise. In this case the court found that a hospital inherently has control over a private independently contracted group of emergency physicians (who were private direct billing physicians) through its basic procedures and control over the facilities in which they practice. Furthermore, because the emergency department was part of the hospital, it created the appearance of a master-servant relationship between the hospital and these physicians.

The courts indicated that the hospital "represented to the decedent that the staff of the hospital emergency room were its employees, thereby causing the decedent to rely on the skill of the emergency staff, and the hospital is consequently liable to the decedent as if the emergency room staff were its employees."

Finally, to appreciate the full impact of the inconsistency of the concept of independent contractor status for hospital-based physicians, the following "Catch 22" is offered: On one hand the hospital-based physician may insist on an independent contractor clause as a demonstration of his professional autonomy within the terms of the contract with the hospital, and the hospital attorney may gladly accept this suggestion. On the other hand, the pathologist, radiologist and other hospital-based physicians may insist that they are ultimately responsible for the supervision and quality of services provided by "their" departments, but they, in fact, share liability with the hospital.

How can an independent contractor be vested with this kind of organizational responsibility? If this is not enough, witness what happens when the hospital tries to invoke the "independent contractor" defense from liability for the negligence of these hospital-based physicians: The courts simply do not accept it. In other words, some hospital administrators and governing boards have very unwisely failed to manifest their right to control these hospital-based physicians without any corresponding relief in the hospital's end liability for their performance.

9. Professional Status Issue

It should be obvious by now that other deep, intangible feelings are also somehow involved in making this whole issue of hospital-based physician contracts so difficult. While financial incentives are probably one key consideration, and the desire to remain independent from the hospital is obviously another, a somewhat more ambiguous factor seems to be exacerbating the resentment against salaried arrangements and other more restrictive contracts with hospitals.

There are a multitude of concerns, but one that should not be underestimated is professional image and status, especially in light of the serious recruiting problems and lack of appeal of these medical specialties.

These hospital-based physicians have obviously been in search of an identity with the medical profession as a whole and even though the A.M.A. accorded them official recognition and acceptance into the fraternity back in the 1920's and 1930's, they apparently have felt that their fellow physicians still do not accept them as medical peers. It is becoming less and less clear that they are independent contractors like other physicians, and no doubt they are not enthralled by being perceived by the courts and fellow physicians as the "servant" in a master/servant relationship with the hospital. As Professors Herman and Anne Somers bluntly put it: "Opinions vary as to whether the inherent conditions of hospital specialist practice are inimical to their relative prestige, but most specialists clearly have not suffered in at least one index of status — income."

Even their high average personal incomes compared with those of the rest of the medical profession, however, still have not won them recognition with their fellow physicians and it now appears that many of these hospital-based physicians have decided that if they cannot actually have a direct relationship with patients, they can at least bill patients directly as other private fee-for-service physicians do.

The newly emerging specialty of hospital-based emergency physicians is also facing this professional image crisis and it, too, is apparently recommending the same solution — direct billing, fee-for-service. At the 1972 Ambulatory Care Workshop of the Institute of Medicine of Chicago, Dr. Ralston Hannas, then president of the American College of Emergency Physicians, said: "We are trying to improve the image of emergency medicine. For many years it was delegated to the lowest man in the pecking order, usually the interns or the residents; sometimes the foreign speaking resident who might be well trained but had very great problems communicating with both the patient and the medical staff."

Dr. Hannas, a strong opponent of salaried emergency physician contracts then went on to say: "A contract, fee-for-service emergency physician arrangement gives the patient an incentive to stay well, and it lets the patient know who is treating him. It is really the physician treating him and not the hospital." Unfortunately, H.E.W.'s Health Care Financing Administration's 1975 study could not evaluate compensation levels for emergency physicians who bill directly (because this information obviously is not available to hospitals), but we do know from this study that salaried emergency physicians earned only slightly more than half what emergency physicians on percentage of revenue arrangements earned ($40,400 *vs.* $74,900) and there is no reason to assume that direct billing would be less than this latter figure.

In the development of hospital-based physician contracts, one physician writer, Dr. Anthony Satillaro, suggested in an article "An Open Approach To Contractual Arrangements" in *The Hospital Medical Staff* (March 1978) that a salary contract may be the preferred option if the physician values his security and "institutional support and protection." If, on the other hand, "He is very concerned with his image among his colleagues, he may choose the fee-for-service approach, which offers optimum patient and colleague contact with usually little control from hospital administration."

It would appear that where hospital administrators were once encouraged — or coerced — to sanction financially open ended contracts, they are now being encouraged to have an open approach to the types of agreements so the hospital-based physicians' needs for security or image can be satisfied.

Another manifestation of the professional status problem is that most hospitals fail to give their chairmen of pathology, radiology and emergency medicine (and others) full recognition and voting status on the medical executive committee. Some hospitals may allow the appointment of one chairman to represent several such "non-clinical" departments. I believe that anything short of full recognition of such key departments on the medical executive committee is counterproductive to good medical organization and decision making. It makes very little difference that the chief pathologist may only have two other staff associates while the chairman of the department of medicine may have 30 members in his department. The policy making body of the medical staff requires, and so should recognize, the important contribution of these departments which can influence the practice and quality of care provided by all physicians on the staff. Perhaps if hospital management and medical staff officers were to recognize this, there might be less unnecessary frustration felt by these specialists over their image and importance.

10. Direct Billing — A Way Out?

Most of the issues or pseudo-issues discussed in this chapter so far provide a historical perspective to the basis for these relationships between hospitals and hospital-based physicians. I have listed some of the serious defects and counter-incentives inherent in percentage of revenue arrangements, which until the early 1970's were the commonest of all those adopted by pathologists and radiologists. It is unfortunate that the trend is toward more and more fee-for-service direct billing and the list of defects in this type of arrangement is longer and even more serious.

Because the percentage of revenue arrangements have resulted in such gross abuse, direct billing may become the most convenient, face saving way out of the problem for both the hospitals and their hospital-based physicians. If, upon completing an area-wide survey of compensation rates, the hospital administrator suddenly finds that his radiologists, on a percentage of gross income, are earning an average of more than $200,000 each, he may wish he had never undertaken the study, for to know how exorbitant the compensation levels are requires a decision to let them continue or to somehow bring them back into line. If these radiologists had been billing directly, with no control by the hospital, the administrator would not know what their earnings were and presumably would be less subject to board or even public censure. After all, no one could blame the administrator if a pediatrician or surgeon in private practice on his staff was charging excessive fees and earning high six digit incomes.

The problem with this logic is, of course, that in so doing the administrator relinquishes a responsibility that automatically goes along with the granting of an exclusive franchise or monopoly, namely, the requirement to regulate charges of the franchise in the absence of normal, open market price competition. It doesn't take a genius to predict what will happen when a monopoly is sanctioned with no price regulation. Nevertheless, as we shall see, there are indeed incentives for an administrator to allow direct billing rather than having to face the more difficult task of renegotiating a contract that is already substantially out of control.

From the physician's point of view, he, too, would just as soon have his income less visible to the public, his fellow physicians, the administrator and the board, and he obviously has a strong incentive to convert his percentage arrangement to direct billing. As a matter of fact, with the trend towards state rate review commissions, we can expect more and more physicians to favor direct billing as a means of keeping their charge structure outside the review process of regulatory agencies.

Direct billing will presumably afford them as much protection as the private-practice physicians currently have. From the hospital-based physician's point of view, combined billing by the hospital for his services (as distinguished from direct billing with no hospital involvement) is not a satisfactory solution because it still leaves his fee vulnerable to regulation by these agencies at some future time and also obviously under constant review by administration and boards of trustees. Also, even direct billing with ultimate authority by the hospital to control fees charged is not a satisfactory solution because this still allows the administration to remain in indirect control of and also privy to the annual earnings of these specialists.

The argument usually put forth by hospital-based physicians as to why they should be allowed to bill directly is simply that they should have the same rights as any other physician, and since the hospital does not attempt to regulate the fees of surgeons who use the hospital's operating suites, the hospital also has no right to regulate the fees charged by radiologists who use its x-ray equipment or emergency physicians who use its emergency room. In addition, it is usually argued that direct billing provides the hospital-based physician an incentive to see more patients or do more interpretations and like other physicians he should be compensated for his extra efforts.

Most professional societies now encourage their memberships to develop direct billing arrangements, and the only hospital-based physician group that will have any difficulty are the pathologists, for whom it becomes nearly impossible to establish a billing and collection service for a half a million or so specific laboratory procedures performed annually. One of the problems with direct billing is that it automatically adds an extra billing and collection cost that previously was absorbed as part of the hospital's established billing process.

In a 1974 study, the cost of generating a second, separate bill was $2 or $3 or roughly from $120,000 to $180,000 extra cost for a hospital that serves 60,000 patients in its x-ray department annually. This type of cost obviously has to be absorbed by someone and it is certainly doubtful whether in a group of five radiologists each would voluntarily take a reduction of about $30,000 annually in his income for the privilege of direct billing; this obviously will be absorbed by the patient through his insurance premiums.

In the same study by the Pennsylvania Insurance Department it was concluded that "a move by physicians to direct billing is unnecessarily and exorbitantly expensive and inefficient. . .and the Insurance Department will explore every avenue open to us to preclude such direct billing." More specifically, the study concluded that ". . .if hospital-based physicians billed directly in accordance with the recommendations of their various associations. . .radiologists would experience a 112 percent increase." By extrapolation we can then say that Dr. Sidney Wolfe's estimate of $215 million in excess compensation in 1975 (when percentage of revenue was most prevalent) would more than double to a figure of roughly $450 million if such physicians converted to direct billing.

H.E.W.'s 1977 Health Care Financing Administration study revealed an even more dramatic case of a 500 percent increase when hospital-based physicians convert to direct billing: "The administrator of one (New York) hospital had specific figures to support his concern. The group of radiologists in his hospital had switched from salary to direct billing in 1972, at the physicians' insistence. In its last full year under a salary arrangement, the group consisted of four hospital-based physicians who were paid a total of less than $150,000. He reported that the same group, now consisting of five hospital-based physicians, had generated gross revenues of $850,000 under the direct billing arrangement."

There are several factors that cause this, including the already mentioned cost of the billing process itself. In addition, as the 1974 Pennsylvania Insurance Department report further indicated, "When the physicians are employed by the hospitals their income is usually tied to the productivity of their departments, whereas in the direct billing situations increases in income can be generated by simple fee increases." There are other factors, too, that make these arrangements uneconomical. Direct billing is inherently inflationary to the extent that fees are set and then revised on the basis of areawide averages, "usual and customary" for the area; that is, a chain reaction effect of fee escalations which may or may not have any relationship to cost of living, scarcity of supply of specialists, or other such factors and such fee escalations are beyond the control or influence of the hospital.

The direct billing arrangement also has virtually all the counter-incentives inherent in the percentage of revenue arrangement, *i.e.* no incentive to discourage unnecessary over-ordering of services, no incentive to improve the efficiency of operations of the department, and no incentive to the specialists to add partners (and, thereby, have to spread their earnings over a larger base) until absolutely necessary.

It is unfortunate there are so many pressures to encourage the direct billing option from the hospital-based physicians, from outside agencies, and even from the hospitals. Aside from the catalyzing effect rate review agencies may have on this, it is quite conceivable that as the legislative bodies finally begin to put the clamps on percentage of revenue arrangements, more hospital-based physicians will attempt to negotiate direct billing arrangements rather than salaries with their administrators, and of course, the specialist societies will fully support these efforts. Surprisingly in the H.C.F.A. study many New York administrators indicated they favored allowing their hospital-based physicians to convert to a direct billing arrangement. According to the study, "This can best be explained by considering that if a hospital has exceeded or is close to exceeding its cost ceiling (under New York's rate review program) it can be in the hospital's best interest to have the hospital-based physicians billing direct."

Currently, the American Hospital Association's *Guidelines on Contractual Arrangements Between Hospitals and Hospital-Based Physicians* does not take a specific position against direct billing but does take the position that the hospital has the right to approve charges under separate billing arrangements and encourages hospitals to do the billing.

HOSPITAL-BASED PHYSICIANS

It should be clear by now that many existing contractual arrangements between hospitals and hospital-based physicians are grossly inadequate, ineffective, uneconomical, and counterproductive and will eventually have to be renegotiated to extricate the physicians (and hospitals) from this situation which has attracted the attention of the public, legislators and some politically-motivated bounty hunters.

As the hospital enters renegotiations (or even first-time negotiations for many of the newly emerging hospital-based physicians) it is important that administrators and trustees fully appreciate not only the medical profession's position in general but also the unique position of hospital-based physicians. However, a good hospital negotiator will go even one step further and attempt to understand the special needs and concerns of each specific group of hospital-based physicians: pathologists, emergency care physicians, cardiologists, radiologists, nuclear physicians, medical administrators and so on. To this extent an effort will be made to address some of the key issues and concerns of these groups, and it is hoped that administrators and governing boards will appreciate the importance of unique contractual arrangements that are specific to the needs of each specialty group.

1. Organized Medicine's Influence

Physicians, in general, like many other professional persons, put a great deal of value on their independence and will fight hard to prevent any encroachments. Any regulatory agency, statute, law or institution that threatens their professional freedom is likely to provoke a surprisingly organized and relentless retaliation — surprising because it is difficult to imagine 500,000 defiantly independent men and women capable of mobilizing for or against any cause for a sustained period of time. The American Medical Association obviously has had its hands full as the representative of organized medicine in this country. Through it, physicians have attempted to stop, postpone or dramatically alter the enactment of the Medicare Act (unsuccessful), the National Health Facilities Planning Act (unsuccessful), the P.S.R.O. Act (unsuccessful) and various national health insurance bills (successful, so far).

The hospital represents a potentially threatening institution — one that could some day interfere with the independent practice status physicians have cherished. More and more physicians are faced with the difficult decision of which devil to bargain with — the government or the hospital. Under the P.S.R.O. Act, hospital medical staffs had the option of keeping the quality control and auditing process within their own institution, either by so called "delegated review" or by allowing an external governmental-approved agency to do the reviewing. Many hospital medical staffs labored over this option for fear they would lose control under either circumstance.

It is not surprising that the trend of judicial decisions, including Darling, Nork, Moore and others, which designate the hospital and its governing body as having ultimate responsibility for ensuring the quality of care (including nonprofessional, professional and medical) practiced in the hospital is of great concern to physicians in private practice. It is likely that many of them are watching very closely to see what happens with the hospital-based physicians who, in a sense, represent quasi-institutionalization of medical practice. Should hospital-based physicians lose all pretense of their independent contractor status, whether by judicial ruling, federal laws such as Medicare and P.S.R.O., or hospital governing boards and administrators exerting their newly defined authorities, this may serve as a harbinger of the future for all physicians who use hospitals in one way or another.

However, even though physicians in general have been supportive of their fellow hospital-based physicians in their efforts to retain professional independence, hospital-based physicians still are not afforded full professional respect by private practitioners (nor for that matter by the public in general). Hospital-based physicians are frequently perceived as ancillary — support staff for the private practitioner — a situation that gives rise to expressions of frustration about their lack of professional esteem and parity with other physicians.

Compounding this problem is the fact that many recent exposes of the high personal earnings hospital-based physicians have generated with their favorable open ended contracts may be causing more than mild envy among private practitioners. Not only are pathologists and radiologists by far the highest paid physicians in this country, but with their exceptional arrangements with hospitals they have had a dramatically faster inflation of their incomes over the past decade than other physicians have. In 1968 the average net income of pathologists and radiologists was close to, though slightly higher than, that of other physicians, *i.e.* $46,360 and $46,423 respectively *vs.* $40,654 for surgeons, for example. By 1975-76 there was a 60 percent spread between the $62,799 incomes for all private practitioners and the $98,000 to $103,000 earnings of pathologists and radiologists.

Also adding to some potential difficulties between private practitioners and hospital-based physicians is the emergence of several new hospital-based specialists who by the nature of their new functions may be in direct competition with primary care physicians.

Back in 1966, even though hospital-based physicians had

no way to assure professional respect from fellow physicians, they at least had their political support. Now, however, not only are the hospital-based physicians a little more reluctant to have staff physicians get involved with or be otherwise exposed to their lucrative arrangements, organized medicine may be a little less inclined to provide the backing it used to give.

A subtle but important and real feature of organized medicine is the unwritten rule for referring a patient from one physician to another, typically from a generalist to a specialist. This may also reflect a basic possessiveness by physicians over "their" patients in the so-called special physician-patient relationship. In particular, where primary care physicians and surgeons are involved, there are usually clearly articulated ethical principles against fee splitting to prevent a referral based solely on a financial kickback. But more subtle is the case in which a physician may be the recipient of referrals based on his special status and implicit authority as a hospital-based physician, such as a part-time salaried chairman of the department of medicine or surgery or pediatrics.

Staff physicians in these departments may resent an excessive number of referrals or consultations going to these hospital-based physicians and may even suggest the imposition of such constraints as not being allowed to affiliate with new partners in their practice, thereby preventing a person employed part-time as clinical chairman from receiving too many referrals and consultation requests. Similarly, the emergency care physician is usually prevented by the hospital medical staff members from retaining admitting privileges at the hospital where they have their emergency practices.

The obvious reason is that such privileges might allow them to admit or otherwise provide follow-up care of a patient who arrives at the emergency room without an established family physician. The same problems may apply to hospital-based cardiologists and respiratory care specialists who might be perceived by fellow private practitioners as exceeding the right to get involved in the management of care of their patients.

Related to this are two quasi-sacred tenets of organized medicine: (1) that patients should always have the right to select their own physicians, and (2) that the American practice of medicine is based on the fee-for-service system under which the patient is billed for specific services rendered. This has long been one of the most inviolable tenets of the profession and explains some of organized medicine's resistance to Health Maintenance Organizations (and other prepaid group arrangements) as well as its long-standing opposition to salaried arrangements with any physicians; although it is now a common practice for even physicians in private practice to pay salaries to junior partners. It is, in fact, remarkable that the American Medical Association ever sanctioned the percentage of revenue arrangements that most hospital-based physicians worked out with hospitals many years ago, for these certainly are not fee-for-service plans. Perhaps this is just another indication that organized medicine had always considered hospital-based physicians less than full members of the medical fraternity. In any case, now both the A.M.A. and the specialty societies fully support the fee-for-service, direct billing arrangements for hospital-based physicians.

Incidentally, it should be pointed out that fee-for-service among private-practice independent contractors no longer has the significance it used to have, something most physicians are reluctantly having to recognize and live with. Direct billing, fee-for-service, in its purest form, worked effectively for physicians before third-party governmental and private insurance reimbursement became commonplace. Not only are fees scrutinized for "reasonableness" by these third party payers, the physician rarely has the privilege any longer of having his bill paid directly by the patient.

If the various state rate review commissions ever get authority to regulate physician fees, the professional privileges inherent in the old fee-for-service method will be lost forever. Thus, organized medicine has a more than passive interest in what will happen with hospital-based physicians in their attempts to keep their professional charges from being classified as hospital services *per se* and thus vulnerable to regulation by rate review commissions.

In another area of physician behavior and attitudes, it is apparent that most physicians feel as enthusiastic about legal matters and lawyers as they do about hospital corporations, planning agencies, and legislators. It is interesting how threatening the law seems to most physicians; they would prefer to have nothing to do with it and the majority are very poorly versed in even the most fundamental medico-legal issues. The malpractice crisis of the mid 1970s and the growing tendency of consumers to file suits against physicians have changed this to some extent, but many physicians still believe such outdated principles as the general rule of locality and local precedence are legitimate defenses in court.

Physicians tend to dislike legal or otherwise binding contracts and prefer more informal agreements. Thus, Dr. Anthony Sattilaro states in the article "An Open Approach To Contractual Arrangements," published in *The Hospital Medical Staff* for March 1978, that "Without some legal training or lengthy experience in negotiations, the physician is at a distinct disadvantage." It is, therefore, probably not surprising that less than 50 percent of hospital-based physicians in this country have formal contracts or agreements with their hospitals, as revealed in the 1977 HCFA study, and that the American College of Radiology was quick to recommend in 1966 that because radiologists should be independent specialists who bill patients directly they need not establish any contracts or agreements at all with hospitals.

The College of American Pathologists took a similar position, and the American Society of Anesthesiologists continued to assume that no contract or agreement was ever necessary. As a compromise, many hospital administrators have received simple letters, so called "intent to assure services," from their specialists in a unilateral decision to make such a letter a substitute for a mutually agreed upon, legally binding contract. One such proposed format for radiologists starts out: "I do not wish to enter into a contract with Golden Rule Hospital because such contracts are neither offered to other members of the medical staff, nor required of other members of the medical staff. I recognize, however, the past relationship I have had with the hospital, and I can, therefore, appreciate the desire of you (the administrator) and the Board for certain assurances in connection with the future availability of services to patients in the hospital."

In spite of the past successes of the majority of hospital-based physicians in avoiding any formal contractual relationship with hospitals, there is a growing awareness by organized medicine of the inevitability of such binding contracts and in 1977 the American Medical Association took the initiative to establish a department of negotiation and is currently sponsoring seminars on the art of negotiating. The *A.M.A. News* (Aug. 4, 1978) editorial encouraged its membership to participate in these programs (at a cost of around $400). The seminars are called "Negotiating: The Dynamics of Conflict Resolution" and their purpose, according to the A.M.A. editorial, is as follows: "The practicing physician must counteract influences (and intrusions that frustrate a physician's exercise of professional judgment) if he is to maintain the quality of care he delivers (and) if he is to retain a professional relationship with his patients."

2. The Hospital-Based Physician's Position

Over and above some of the general needs and concerns of the medical profession as a whole, the hospital-based physicians have some unique concerns and problems of their own that hospital executives should keep in mind.

Foremost, as we have suggested, may be the problem of professional prestige and parity with other physicians. It is apparent that all the following strategies have still not given hospital-based physicians the peer respect they desire or need:

1. Official recognition in 1924 and 1939 by the A.M.A. that radiology and pathology, respectively, were part of the practice of medicine.
2. Retention of "independent contractor" clauses in most contracts with hospitals.
3. Recognition that they indirectly were reimbursable under Medicare as a "medical service" (Part B) rather than exclusively as a "hospital service" (Part A).
4. Partial and reluctant acceptance by one state review commission in 1978 that their services are not strictly part of the hospital's costs and charges, and that their fees may fall outside rate review commission regulation, like fees of other doctors.
5. Extraordinarily high personal compensations that could be expected to accrue to the most competent individuals in the profession.

In this search by the hospital-based physicians for professional recognition there have been some strategies that failed, including the failure in several court rulings to obtain recognition for their services as truly "diagnostic" and the J.C.A.H.'s unwillingness to view their services as a form of consultation to fellow physicians. Also, the corporate practice of medicine statute has provided only limited, and now waning, support; and even though most hospitals still allow them to keep their independent contractor clauses in their agreements, the courts have consistently called them "servants" in the principle of *Respondeat Superior.*

In 1966 some formerly contented hospital-based physicians, notably the radiologists, declared their desire to be independent of the hospital and to denounce their percentage of revenue contracts as if these had made them indentured servants. As a matter of fact, most hospital-based physicians probably had good, amiable relationships with their hospitals prior to 1966, and in many cases they served as an important bridge between the medical staff as a whole and management because they were capable of identifying with both the corporate entity and also the medical staff.

Hospital-based physicians frequently are significantly more sophisticated about financial, legal and management issues than is the independent practitioner, and have a relatively better understanding of the need for an organizational process and corporate accountability. Because of the urgings of their professional societies in 1965 and 1966, unfortunately, some specialists felt obliged to sever their close relationships with their hospitals, and to this day many hospital-based physicians are still trying to decide if they are part of management or part of the medical staff — a tragic dilemma when no such distinctions were really necessary or even relevant. In any case, contract negotiators should be aware of this somewhat schizophrenic posture that some specialists may have, especially in view of the fact that theirs' is a symbiotic relationship with the hospital and they cannot function outside of it.

No matter how much it is desired, a compromise is not always reached by just two parties, the buyer and the seller, but may be affected more by the market or the situation the parties are in at the time of the transaction. Similarly, we should appreciate the fact that both the hospital and hospital-based physician cannot deal with each other in a vacuum. Although a hospital-based physician may have been amenable all along to a fair salary arrangement, he may now have to worry about how this will be perceived by his fellow specialists at neighboring hospitals. If such a concession to management might clearly serve as an areawide precedent, he is risking the wrath of his neighboring specialists. This is why a hospital-based physician brought in from another area might be more willing to accept such arrangements without overwhelming concern about peer pressure from colleagues he does not even know personally.

Also, no matter how loyal and committed the hospital-based physician may be to his hospital, and, therefore, willing to work under a reasonable contract, he still will have some loyalties to his professional society and as a member in good standing he may be reluctant to go too far astray from its principles and opinions on types of contractual arrangements. The professional specialist societies do have a valuable role to play and it is not entirely self-serving. Hospitals are in a position to exert virtually absolute control over specialized human resources (nurses, technicians, and hospital-based physicians) who are so specialized they don't have much freedom to use their skills in other industries, even if their hospital compensation or work conditions are intolerable. As a consequence, hospitals could easily exploit specialized resources for their own greater profits. Hence, unions and professional societies are important in protecting their membership from potential abuse.

Specialist societies also fit into the negotiation process to the extent that they encourage unified behavior by their membership in support of positions and principles for their own benefit. Now that some of these positions have been declared violations of anti-trust laws, specialist societies (as well as the A.M.A.) have resorted to a new educational strategy. If the specialist societies are prohibited from price fixing or explicit efforts to discourage salaried arrangements, they can legally educate (almost to the point of indoctrination) their members to the benefits of percentage of revenue and direct billing arrangements, and also provide them with effective negotiating skills to resist hospital management's efforts.

While it may be rare for two orthopedic surgeons to compare notes on their personal incomes, it is not uncommon for two pathologists in neighboring hospitals to discuss the arrangements they have with their respective hospitals and, thereby, indirectly reveal compensation data. This has two consequences worth considering in regard to the hospital-based physician's negotiating position.

First, even if a chief radiologist believes that he is fairly compensated at, say, $100,000 a year, when he hears from his colleagues at other hospitals that they receive $200,000 or $300,000, he may well begin to think he is under-compensated in comparison with these local market conditions or that the nature of his contract prevents him from earning what his fellow specialists earn. So, while he may not have been inherently unhappy with his arrangement, more and more, he begins to feel he is allowing himself to be cheated. The second factor of importance is that he may cite the earnings of his colleagues during the negotiation process to bargain up to what he perceives to be his market value. The problem with this, of course, is that local area compensation levels usually have very little to do with true market value of these specialists, but rather are an indication of the irresponsibility shown by the managements of these neighboring hospitals for allowing such contracts.

Another important consideration with hospital-based physicians is the underlying confusion over the medical versus administrative skills their job may require, and, as we know, many courts and regulatory agencies have also floundered over this point. Basically, the question is: Does the practice of medicine include professional, technical and administrative services as well as clinical services? There may be little point in laboring this issue, but unless these distinctions are made somewhere in the contract negotiation process, loss of clear-cut accountability and inequitable compensations will result.

If the chief pathologist and his associates are expected to have direct administrative and supervisory responsibilities over the various sections of the laboratory, this should be made clear, and management should satisfy itself that these pathologists have the necessary personal and professional capabilities to supervise and manage. So, too, if radiologists are expected to supervise technicians, this should be defined. The chiefs of these services should also have clearly defined administrative responsibilities and they should be qualified to fulfill these functions with corresponding remuneration for this administrative duty.

Not nearly enough attention is paid to this distinction between management and clinical requirements by most hospitals — almost as if it is assumed that all hospital-based physicians are inherently endowed with management skills. The typical 300 to 400 bed hospital in this country may have up to 10 percent of all its full-time equivalent employees in the two departments of x-ray and laboratory, and more than 10 percent of its total operating expenses attributable to those departments, and yet not consider adequately the administrative and management skills of these department chiefs.

Rarely do the professional societies speak to this. The American College of Radiology's October 1965 *Bulletin* simply says: "Appointment of radiologists to a hospital staff should be based upon the same criteria of personal competence and need for service as used for other members of the medical staff." But hospitals do not typically give to family practitioners, pediatricians and others authority to make decisions that affect $2 million or more of the hospital's annual operating expenses. Pity the poor administrator who has inherited a chief radiologist or chief anesthesiologist who cannot even effectively manage his associates, much less the paraprofessional staff in these departments. It is not likely that he will be able to turn to a contract with these individuals that spells out the chief's specific responsibility for effective administration and management of his department, his staff and the department's resources. In most such departments it is not very difficult to find poor management practices — including inconsistent purchasing practices (e.g. noncompetitive bidding for annual orders of up to $500,000 of x-ray films and favored suppliers), poor personnel practices (special bonuses and other benefits contrary to hospital policy), and inadequate financial controls (e.g. no controls over lost or late charges). More and more hospitals are recognizing the need for hospital-employed departmental managers to counteract these management deficiencies.

No doubt, most hospital-based specialists enjoy running their own departments. They tend to be possessive and defensive about their departments and their employees. It is not surprising that laboratory and x-ray personnel in many departments appear somewhat isolated from the mainstream of the hospital. Frequently, these are the least active group in hospital sponsored activities such as the bowling league. They tend to identify more with the laboratory and their chief than the hospital as a whole. Most chiefs think they have well-run departments and loyal staffs.

In summary, we now have a picture of some of the motivations and concerns of hospital-based physicians in general, including:

1. A need or desire for professional recognition and status among other physicians.

2. An inherently conflicting desire to be independent from control by the hospital, while at the same time a need to be dependent on the hospital to provide the necessary resources to fulfill his function.

3. An ability to appreciate hospital and institutional objectives and priorities and also an understanding of the demands and needs of the medical profession in general and his specialty societies in particular.

4. A desire to stay competitive in his earnings with fellow specialists in his area.

5. Administrative and managerial requirements and a desire to run his own department with as much independence as possible from the rest of the hospital organization.

The professional recognition issue is probably the strongest motivation of all, and even though other issues may arise it is possible that these are all manifestations of this one. If professional prestige and recognition have been critical motivations of hospital-based physicians, one may now be wondering to what extent personal economic incentives are behind this.

Is money the real issue, especially in light of the incomes these hospital-based physicians have achieved?

It is probably true also that in a one-to-one contract negotiation session between a hospital-based physician and a hospital, human nature would dictate an effort to ensure the highest possible personal gain, and in this sense during individual negotiations the bottom line dollar is probably the critical issue, no matter what other apparent issues are put forth. Now if the contract eventually proves to be "too rewarding" (a circumstance, unfortunately, not too many of us can appreciate from our side of the fence), we can also expect that the hospital-based physician will not voluntarily refund some of his earnings. This is an understandable and human characteristic that suggests hospitals should not enter agreements that put some physicians in this kind of a situation.

In my opinion, hospital-based physicians did not set out to be the medical profession's highest paid physicians. Rather, as was aptly put by Dr. Kenneth Williams "Medicine's New Royalists," Feb. 4, 1973: "These types of situations that I describe as scandalous — where pathologists, radiologists and other hospital-based physicians have such exorbitant contracts, up into six figures — exist only because the hospital trustees and management allow them to exist." (Dr. Williams is former vice president of medical affairs of the Catholic Hospital Association and former medical administrator of St. John Hospital in Detroit).

Nobody looks good when agreements permit individual physicians to earn huge sums.

3. Hospital-Based Physician Concerns and Contract Needs

Many years ago there were basically only three types of hospital-based physicians who had contractual relationships with hospitals — pathologists, radiologists and anesthesiologists. Then came the cardiologists to perform electrocardiograph interpretations as the specialty of cardiology became more sophisticated, and they have been followed by neurologists, pulmonary medicine specialists and many others who assist in diagnosis through interpretations of various test results.

In the last 10 years we have seen the emergence of several other specialists including the nuclear physicians, physiatrists, nephrologists, neonatologists, infectious disease experts, and even a group of hospital-based physicians who are specialists in one sense but generalists in another. These are the emergency care physicians who are trained to handle acute, episodic illnesses but must also be capable of diagnosing and managing, if only temporarily, all ranges of medical, obstetrical, pediatric, psychiatric and surgical problems.

If this is not enough of an increase in hospital-based physicians, we now have a whole new breed coming onto the scene in response to several legislative mandates, judicial decisions, and the changing role of the hospital, and this group includes medical administrators under contract with the hospital — medical directors, clinical department chairmen, directors of medical education, utilization review coordinators, directors of critical care units and specialty care units among others. One community hospital in the Midwest (with 400 beds and 200 staff physicians) has gone from 10 to 59 physicians under contract with the hospital (part-time and full-time) in just six years — representing 30 full-time equivalent hospital-based physicians and involving 16 different specialties.

The point, however, is that when one is dealing with 16 different specialty groups of hospital-based physicians, it may be necessary to provide an equal number of different contractual arrangements instead of simply trying to force a percentage of revenue or salary arrangement to work in all cases. As a matter of fact, it was probably wrong ever to expect the percentage of revenue arrangements to apply equally well for pathologists, radiologists and anesthesiologists and this may explain some of our current problems.

Obviously, radiologists and anesthesiologists should earn income in proportion to their personal efforts and the revenue-sharing contracts may have been more reasonable for them, whereas this was never the case with pathologists. Similarly, other variables, aside from the relationship between professional work effort and volume, may be relevant considerations in determining the ideal contract for each specialty. These might include: degree of direct patient contact, specialty training and certification required, clinical and nonclinical skills required, time commitment required, degree of dependence on hospital capital and manpower to perform their functions, and degree of dependence on the hospital and hospital medical staff for referring patients to them.

To achieve the best contractual arrangement, a good hospital negotiator should acquaint himself with the special interests and concerns of each specialty group, because some of these may represent deep-seated biases which, if they go unrecognized, could fog the real issues during the contract negotiation process, especially when there is a vested interest or a status issue at stake.

For the following 10 groups of hospital-based physicians, both the real concerns and issues as well as the potential underlying biases and self-interest motivations will be explored. The comments referred to as "note" after some sections are suggestions for consideration in the contract negotiaation process.

3.1. Pathologists

Inasmuch as pathologists (and radiologists) have been covered fairly extensively in Chapter I, the following will only serve as a summary of some of their key concerns, issues, and biases as they might relate to contract negotiations.

(a) In their symbiotic relationship with the hospital, pathologists are probably the most dependent of all hospital-based physicians; they need the hospital for referral of work and they need its equipment and technical staff to carry out this work.

Note: Pathologists may not like the connotation of "servant" in the master-servant relationship with the hospital, but the reality of this relationship is clear in practice and in the courts.

(b) Pathologists have few direct patient contacts, and thus few traditional physician-patient relationship; nor do patients have any choice in the selection of pathologists.

(c) Pathologists are typically involved directly in only about 10 percent of the output of their departments (surgical pathologic analyses, autopsies), and are expected to provide clinical supervision over all other laboratory output.

Note: Contracts should clearly define this supervision responsibility and pathologists should be evaluated on their ability to provide supervision over the technical staff; also, obviously, contracts should not allow compensation in relation to the entire department's output.

(d) Some pathologists suffer from an anxiety over their image, especially with their fellow physicians, but also with the public. Obtaining peer status with other physicians may be a subtle, but strong, issue.

Note: A simple and correct solution would be to include the pathologists, with full voting privileges, on the hospital's medical executive committee, and appointment to other key medical staff, administration and board committees that have typically been reserved for other clinical department chairmen only.

(e) Pathologists have a strong and active professional society in the College of American Pathologists, which is not reluctant to take a strong defense position on behalf of individual pathologists.

(f) Based on past practices, pathologists tend to favor percentage of revenue arrangements, with leasing a second preferred choice. Fee-for-service direct billing is generally too complicated and costly to be a serious option for pathologists. Salaried arrangements are not favored by the C.A.P. and many pathologists.

Note: In light of the prevalence of percentage of revenue contracts with pathologists, especially on the West Coast, it will usually be difficult (but not impossible) for the hospital negotiator to ignore local areawide precedents on this matter.

(g) Most pathologists have become accustomed to very high personal incomes because of the escalating nature of their existing compensation arrangements.

Note: This will make it extremely difficult for hospital negotiators to make contract revisions that yield any substantial cutbacks, and also difficult to convert to straight salaries because the income levels may already be so high that the governing board may be reluctant to officially sanction such salaries. However, the high income levels of pathologists are also known to many private practitioners and, consequently, pathologists can no longer be assured of support from this latter group in their negotiations with the hospital.

(h) Pathologists are currently anxious about their professional fees coming under the review and control of rate setting commissions, as a hospital service.

Note: They may, therefore, begin to show a strong preference for lease arrangements in an effort to get outside such review processes.

(i) Pathologists enjoy their special relationship with the laboratory staff and tend to view the laboratory as their own private enterprise as distinguished from a hospital department.

Note: Although this typically means a strong loyalty on the part of the technical staff to their pathologists, it also frequently results in inconsistent personnel, purchasing and financial practices in the laboratory, to the detriment of the hospital as a whole.

(j) Since 80 percent or more of the laboratory work performed in most community hospitals relates to inpatient-generated referrals (*vs.* private office or outpatient referrals), hospital-based pathologists are almost completely dependent upon demand controlled by the hospital and its attending staff. Physicians in their offices can draw their own samples on ambulatory patients and either perform simple tests themselves or send the samples to private reference laboratories in preference to the more expensive hospital laboratory. Most third-party reimbursers will not sanction differential charge structures for identical services rendered on an outpatient versus inpatient basis (or any other form of price discrimination) and the pathologists therefore have very little incentive to keep their professional fees competitive with either private reference laboratories or those in other hospitals.

(k) Pathologists have only limited options to sell their service and skills outside the hospital industry. They might operate a private, free-standing reference laboratory, but these opportunities are not abundant. Nevertheless, the pathologist may insist upon his right to operate his own private laboratory if he so desires, if for no other reason than to assure himself that he is not totally dependent on the hospital.

3.2. Radiologists

Basically most of the same points that apply to pathologists also apply to radiologists. They have a strong dependency on the hospital, primarily because of the extensive capital investments required to provide radiology services; they have limited contacts with patients, except in certain special procedures and radiation therapies; they also have an image or status problem; are extremely well-compensated; they have a strong professional society in the American College of Radiology, and, like pathologists, usually have a close working relationship with their technologists and regard the x-ray department as their private domain.

However, there are some notable differences between radiologists and pathologists and these are issues that should be considered relevant only to radiologists:

(a) Every x-ray procedure requires a radiologist's professional interpretation (excluding some procedures performed as part of Nuclear Medicine); therefore, their department's output relates directly to their own professional efforts and skills.

Note: Contract negotiations should somehow take account of this relation to volume, and also of the potential abuse of too few radiologists trying to interpret too many x-rays for their own financial benefit. Typically, the professional societies offer ambiguous guidelines on the reasonable number of physicians required for a given output (e.g. x-ray interpretations), and rules of thumb or areawide averages may have to be used as the basis for determining reasonable staffing. Historical staffing may also be very useful. For example, the hospital negotiator could effectively argue that if two radiologists were performing 36,000 procedures five years ago, no fewer than four radiologists should be required for 72,000 procedures now if the quality is to remain the same.

(b) Radiologists are now favoring separate fee-for-service billing and, more specifically, direct billing as opposed to their traditional percentage of revenue arrangements. Even the A.C.R. took this position in 1966. Although it is virtually an accountant's nightmare to have to separate out and directly bill, say, 80,000 x-ray procedures annually, it is not impossible and not totally uneconomical to do so, as is the case with pathologists who try to directly bill a quarter of a million procedures annually.

Note: Numerous arguments against direct billing have already been mentioned but one that is worth reiterating here is the fact that a private collection agency under contract to the radiologists will significantly increase the cost of hospital care because this new form of overhead has to be absorbed by someone, *i.e.* the patients. In addition, the further development of more and more rate review commissions will probably fuel the movement toward direct billing before the radiologist's fees get caught in this type of review and rate setting process as part of a hospital service.

(c) Perhaps most important is the technological explosion that is broadening the range of radiologists' diagnostic capabilities and in the process diversifying their sources of income beyond traditional x-ray interpretations; these include, in particular, ultrasound, thermography and a whole range of computerized axial tomography services. Nuclear medicine diagnostic services have also grown dramatically as we shall see.

A radiologist who can offer computerized axial tomography services in his department has a competitive edge over neighboring hospitals that do not provide this service, and can, therefore, increase the demand for his professional services.

Note: From the hospital's point of view, this technological explosion and the subsequent increase in demand for these additional diagnostic scanning services may, in fact, make negotiations easier because the radiologists, unlike pathologists, have a whole new range of services they can provide — assuming the hospital is prepared to make the necessary major capital investments, and depending upon the state planning commission's approval of the hospital's request to purchase this equipment.

(d) Although radiologists may be somewhat less dependent on the hospital for referrals of patients as compared with pathologists, the radiologist is more dependent on the hospital for major capital acquisitions. A radiology department may cost several million dollars to construct and properly equip.

Note: It is not surprising that some radiologists may offer to purchase some (but not all) major capital items for their department, even as a "donation" to the hospital. This probably represents their desire to be, or appear to be, less dependent on the hospital for their capital requirements. A naive administrator will allow his radiologists to purchase some of their own equipment directly and later find himself at a negotiating disadvantage on at least two counts: being allowed to purchase some of his own equipment reinforces the specialists argument that this department is his independent enterprise, and also these donations may be cited as a defense of his high professional income.

(e) Many community hospital radiology departments may rely on a fair proportion of outpatient referrals and perhaps as little as 50 percent of their volume from inpatients. In contrast to the situation with pathologists, the local private physicians may be more likely to refer their office patients to the hospital's radiology department for x-rays than to the hospital for laboratory tests because most physicians cannot afford to purchase their own x-ray equipment. Also, the patient has to go where he is to be x-rayed, while in the case of laboratory work, a sample can be sent to a distant private reference laboratory. The radiologist, therefore, has to be somewhat price competitive with both neighboring hospitals and local private, free standing x-ray facilities. This is only true to the extent that referring physicians are price conscious on behalf of their patients. In any case, because the radiologist is not so dependent as the pathologist on inpatient referrals, the hospital radiologist may receive more outpatient x-ray referrals as he lowers his professional charges.

(f) For similar reasons as were cited for pathologists, radiologists usually like to retain an option in their contracts to operate independent practices outside the hospital.

Note: Obviously, if there are no restrictions on the proximity of such private practices to the hospital, the radiologist could compete with the hospital itself for referrals of outpatients. Although this would at first appear to be counterproductive, if his profit margins are greater with his private facility, he will obviously benefit by this competition.

3.3. Emergency Care Physicians

Emergency care physicians constitute one of the most rapidly growing groups of hospital-based physicians and perhaps more than any other they need to establish their new professional identity. However, their problem is not just the question of professional image (like that of radiologists and pathologists); nor is it just a question of obtaining recognition of their newly emerging specialty. It is all this, plus the problem of not alienating many other specialties and other physicians.

There are several reasons why emergency medicine is developing so rapidly. A more mobile society means that fewer people stay long enough in one area to establish a traditional relationship with a primary care physician, and thus come to depend upon their local hospital emergency department to meet some of their episodic primary care health needs; this is true particularly in the nonrural areas of the country. Also the hospital itself has gradually assumed a larger role in the delivery of health care over the past 20 years and emergency services are becoming just another form of outpatient or ambulatory care for the public it serves.

Many state legislations now require hospitals to provide more comprehensive emergency services than ever before. Improved insurance coverage for emergency care (and other outpatient services) may also provide some incentive for the public to go to a hospital emergency department rather than a private practitioner's office. In the 1970 Joint Commission on Accreditation of Hospitals standards, the following recommendation was added: "There should be a chief of emergency service who is a member of the active medical staff and who implements the policies and supervises the professional medical services," thereby, giving further credence to this specialty.

To respond to this growing demand on hospital emergency departments, three common emergency physician staffing plans emerged in the early 1960's and this has some influence on current practices and contractual arrangements. The Pontiac (Michigan) Plan was one in which a group of hospital staff physicians (in various specialties) agreed to serve in the emergency room on part time assigned rotations. They retained their existing practices and for their time and service in the emergency department they were allowed to directly bill emergency patients, or otherwise were reimbursed for their services from the corporation of such part-time emergency physicians.

Another approach, called the Alexandria (Virginia) Plan was developed by a private practitioner who simply moved his practice into the emergency room and limited his private practice to full-time emergency care.

This plan, too, was perceived as a private-fee-for service, direct billing arrangement in most instances where it was adopted. A third pattern was simply to contract with a physician's placement bureau to provide part-time or moonlighter doctors to cover the hospital's emergency department throughout all required shifts. Prior to the development of such plans, emergency room coverage was provided on a hit-or-miss basis by volunteer members of the medical staff as a whole, or by moonlighting residents, or new members of the staff trying to build up a practice from their service in the emergency department.

With this background we can now appreciate some of the special needs and concerns of hospital-based emergency physicians:

1. Variations of the Alexandria Plan are the preferred approaches to emergency service and the A.M.A. has endorsed the model, under which the hospital contracts with an incorporated group of emergency physicians. Based on a 1973 survey by the American College of Emergency Physicians, 65 percent of its membership practiced in a group or corporate arrangement and independently of the hospital on a fee-for-service basis. The A.C.E.P. also supports fee-for-service and direct billing as opposed to salaries.

2. As more and more hospitals convert from a voluntarily staffed emergency department or otherwise provide hospital-based emergency care physician coverage, the commonest conversion route is to provide these physicians with a minimum-guarantee contract, whereby the hospital either pays a basic salary as a minimum guarantee of income to the physician or guarantees to make up any difference between what the emergency physician collects from patients and an agreed upon compensation level. This arrangement presumably minimizes the risk to emergency physicians if the volume of patients is not sufficient to provide adequate earnings while at the same time avoiding straight salaried arrangements. Eventually when the volume is sufficient, emergency physician groups then may convert to complete fee-for-service direct billing arrangements.

Note: All the inherent problems with direct billing apply here, but, in addition, in 1975 the Bureau of Health Insurance interpreted Section 2109 of the Provider Reimbursement Manual (HIM-15 Section) to exclude certain such guarantee arrangements as Medicare-allowable costs for the hospital. If a hospital guarantees and pays an emergency physician $30,000, and if the emergency physician earns an additional $30,000 through his billing of emergency patients, for a total income of $60,000, the hospital's $30,000 expense is not considered an allowable cost by the B.H.I. Thus, the hospital would have been wiser to make a simple salary payment of $60,000 and not allow any direct billing by the physician because then the entire $60,000 would be an allowable cost. This is critical for hospitals with high Medicare and Medicaid patient loads.

3. The prevalence of this "minimum guarantee" arrangement also probably relates to the fact that the hospital emergency department operates 24 hours, 7 days a week and the volume of patients a physician would see on the night shift may never be sufficient to compensate him adequately on direct billing, or services at night would have to be priced higher than other shifts.

4. Like radiologists and most other hospital-based physicians, the work efforts of emergency care physicians do relate to the volume of output of the department (except as noted above), and although some incentive for work effort is warranted, there is also the risk of too few physicians trying to manage more emergency cases than is appropriate in the interest of their personal economic gain.

5. The most critical concern of emergency physicians relates to their need to establish some place and identity in the medical field. As noted earlier, the American College of Emergency Physicians, which came into being in 1968, defined emergency medicine as a broad "horizontally-based" specialty encompassing a breadth of medical services rather than a concentration in depth like other specialties. This includes their diagnosis and initial treatment of cardiac problems, respiratory problems, fractures, emergency deliveries, acute infections, drug overdoses and reactions, burns and just about anything that can come into the emergency department.

As recently as 1974, however, (in the Feb. 1, 1974, issue of *Medical World News*), the director of the Trauma Division of the American College of Surgeons was quoted as saying:

"Treatment of patients with any and all kinds of conditions in an emergency department does not constitute the practice of a medical specialty, and physicians practicing full time in the locale (the emergency department) are not medical specialists."

Not only has this concept of specializing in breadth been threatening to surgeons, who have traditionally had control over emergency services because of the amount of trauma involved, but it has also been threatening to primary care physicians (pediatricians, general practitioners, and internists), who may feel their practices will be encroached upon by the hospital-based emergency physicians serving in a primary care role.

As a consequence, hospital administration may find some surprising resistance to the establishment of a full-fledged emergency department, and, once established, some extraordinary limitations may be imposed on it by the medical staff. Typically, emergency physicians will be denied admission privileges at the hospital with which they have contracted for emergency services —as a means of ensuring that they do not make self-referrals of unassigned patients or otherwise "steal" another physician's private patients.

For the same reason, many medical staffs will restrict the emergency physicians from proceeding with any treatment of their private patients who arrive at the emergency department until after the private practitioner has been advised the patient is at the hospital and what the apparent problem is. Again, the medical staff may even subtly encourage high professional fees by the emergency physicians so the emergency department does not become a less costly substitute to a physician's private office.

All these constraints on the emergency care physicians may so compromise their ability to carry out their functions effectively that the hospital won't be able to include any substantial clinical responsibilities in their contracts and these physicians will have even more limited opportunities to establish their role as a viable specialty.

Note: For these reasons, a hospital management would be well advised not to permit the hospital's medical staff to exert excessive influence in the contract negotiation process with emergency care physicians, although there is no question that some of these constraints are legitimate, as for example, the potential of self-referrals if they have admitting privileges. The hospital would also be well advised to include in the contract a provision that the emergency department chief serve on the Medical Executive Committee to legitimize his status in the organization and to ensure that policy decisions involving major clinical departments are not unilaterally imposed on the emergency department.

6. As of the late 1970's, this field had still not obtained approval to establish Board Certification in this specialty, even though more than 20 emergency care residency programs have already been established throughout the country. The supply part of the equation has not yet been restricted and it is not expected to for many years; that is, ACEP board certification won't be a prerequisite for emergency physicians (to the exclusion of other specialists) and this cannot, at this time, be used as a bargaining issue by such physicians.

7. Perhaps, like other hospital-based physicians, the emergency physician may be favoring fee-for-service direct billing as an indication of their peer status with other private practitioners. The field of emergency medicine has suffered an image problem; it was usually a duty that fell to residents, moonlighting or otherwise, foreign medical graduates and semi-retired physicians, and most of these physicians were on salary with the hospital for these services. Unlike pathologists and radiologists, however, there is no question that the emergency care physician and the patient do have a direct relationship, albeit limited to one degree or another when it involves another private practitioner's patient. Thus, there may be a stronger basis for their argument that they should be allowed to bill directly.

8. The emergency patient, however, does not have a free choice of physician, and the emergency physician cannot carry out his functions in the absence of all the diagnostic and nursing support services that only the hospital can provide. So, too, the hospital absorbs all the financial risks of fluctuating

demand and bad debts, and also the legal risks for the quality of care rendered in the emergency room. The recent Maryland case of Mehlman *v.* Powell (1977) referred to in Chapter I found the hospital responsible for the performance of its independent, direct-billing emergency physicians on the basis that such physicians practicing in the hospital's emergency department reasonably appeared to the public to be employees of the institution. Incidentally, there is no question that the hospital's emergency department is one of the institution's most critical public image areas as the first and sometimes only point of contact with the hospital by some of its community residents, and in view of the fact that apparently the public perceives emergency physicians as hospital employed, it obviously becomes critical that those retained for these positions be of the highest quality.

9. Many administrators may have indirectly reinforced the A.C.E.P. argument against salaried arrangements by not being more responsive in offering good highly competitive compensation packages. The 1977 H.C.F.A. study of emergency physician incomes in 1975 revealed an average of $55,000, but significantly lower average incomes ($40,000) for those who work under salaried arrangements with hospitals.

3.4 Anesthesiologists

Anesthesiologists are somewhat different from radiologists and pathologists in several respects, and as a result their contractual relationships have been significantly different, including methods of reimbursement. Most anesthesiologists in this country do not have any kind of formal contract with their hospital and most operate on fees for service, either by direct billing or by combined billing by the hospital for the anesthesiologist. The anesthesiologists have been notably absent from the series of conflicts that pathologists and radiologists have had with the Social Security Administration over Medicare and also the rate review commissions. For various reasons they do not perceive themselves, nor apparently are they so perceived by regulatory agencies, as purely hospital-based specialists like radiologists and pathologists.

Here are some of their special concerns and issues.

1. Even though they must depend upon the hospital facilities and nursing staff to provide their special services, the demand for anaesthesia services is not really controlled by the hospital or the medical staff as a whole, but rather by one specific group of physicians, *i.e.* the surgeons, including gynecologists and other subspecialties. To some extent, therefore, the anesthesiologist may not feel the same critical symbiotic relationship with the hospital and it is interesting to note the American Society of Anesthesiologist's Principle I in its 1963 *Statement of Policy:* "The practice of anesthesiology by a member of this Society is the practice of medicine and is not an institutional service."

2. Going one step further, the anesthesiologist is typically considered subservient to the demands of the surgeons, who by some old legal doctrines have been perceived as the "captain of the ship" in the operating suite. According to Henry Beecher in "Trends in Anaesthesia" published in the April 7, 1962, *Journal of the American Medical Association,* it is generally recognized that "the man whose patient is being treated has the right, the obligation to make final decisions." It is not surprising that in most hospitals the surgeon has the right (officially or unofficially) to select the specific anesthesiologist he wants on his case and in most hospitals anesthesiology is considered a section of the department of surgery rather than a free standing department on its own.

Note: For this reason it may be very important in any contractual arrangement to confirm what authority the anesthesiologists have as opposed to those of surgeons, such as who has choice of anaesthetic agents, who determines whether the patient's condition is stable enough to tolerate anesthesia, and several other critical factors.

3. Several court decisions, however, have confirmed that anesthesiologists are independent contractors, or at least independent of the decisions made by the surgeons, as they have been found liable for their own negligence in several cases (see C. E. Wasmuth's *Anaesthesia and the Law,* published in 1961 by C. C. Thomas, Springfield, Ill.).

4. Like emergency care physicians but unlike pathologists and radiologists, anesthesiologists do, in fact, have direct patient relationships, even though patients do not have a free choice of anesthesiologists. Typically, the anesthesiologist not only administers the anaesthetic, but also sees the patient on a preoperative visit, gives preoperative and postoperative physical examinations and determines if the procedures can proceed safely and with what anaesthetic agent.

Note: Any contractual relationship should spell out clearly what the anesthesiologist's obligations are, over and above simply giving an anaesthetic during an operation.

5. Also, unlike pathologists and radiologists, the anesthesiologist does not require major equipment support from the hospital and even his dependence on nurses is relatively minor. All he basically needs from the hospital is the right, the exclusive right, to practice his specialty, in conjunction with the surgeons, in the operating suites of the hospital.

6. As recently as 1978, the Federal Trade Commission came out against the A.S.A.'s position against salaried contracts, on the basis that this constituted restraint of trade and limited competition among anesthesiologists, thereby depriving consumers of the benefit of such competition. It is not surprising however, that the A.S.A.'s position all along favored fee-for-service and its 1963 *Statement of Policy* indirectly even discouraged combined billing by the hospital (in favor of direct billing):

Section V reads: "A member of this Society shall not enter into or remain in any relationship whereby his professional services are offered for a fee . . . except (by) organizations where ownership and management are exclusively in the hands of physicians." This effectively precluded the hospital from such billing until the 1978 F.T.C. position which now requires the A.S.A. to advise its membership that they can use whatever reimbursement arrangement they prefer.

7. Anesthesiologists have a few unique concerns or potential concerns. One of these is the fact anesthesiologists have a nonmedical competitor in nurse anesthetists, and the Joint

Commission on Accreditation of Hospitals does not require a specialist physician in charge of the hospital's anesthesia services. Rather, the standards on this matter simply state: "Anesthesia services shall be organized, directed and integrated with other services or departments of the hospital," and under the J.C.A.H. interpretation of this standard "Anesthesia services shall be directed by a physician member of the medical staff, who shall have over-all administrative responsibilities." This can be any member of the medical staff.

Note: In effect, this enhances the hospital negotiator's bargaining position to the extent that should all else fail in the negotiations, the hospital can employ nurse anaesthetists.

8. Although an anesthesiologist's professional skills and time involvement relates to the volume of output of their services (expressed either on a per case basis or the duration of the procedure), the possible incentive to have too few anesthesiologists and, therefore, increase the personal incomes of each one on the staff is probably not so serious a problem because the staffing is basically determined by the operating rooms available and the demands of the surgeons to provide adequate availability and coverage. It is possible, however, that instead of increasing the number of anesthesiologists as volume of procedures increase, the current staff may attempt to contract with nurse anesthetists (on much lower salaries) to handle this workload and thus they do not compromise current earnings of each anesthesiologist. The hospital negotiator should be alert to this possible ploy.

9. Until only recently, anesthesiologists had virtually no employment opportunities outside hospitals, and, therefore, were exclusively hospital-based. Beginning in the late 1960's, however, a new opportunity emerged with the rapid development of free-standing, private "surgicenters" or same day surgery facilities independent of the hospital.

Note: This obviously enhances this specialist's bargaining power and he may even participate in a private venture close to the hospital that might serve as direct competition to it.

10. Anesthesiologists have one additional opportunity to diversify their sources of income and this involves the poten-

tial participation in pulmonary function — inhalation therapy — respiratory care services of the hospital. The hospital may appoint its anesthesiologist to serve as a consultant to this department or may allow the anesthesiologist the privilege of providing respiratory care consultations.

3.5. Nephrologists

Nephrologists do not suffer from any of the image and status problems of the aforementioned four groups. They also have direct patient contacts, are a recognized board certified specialty and in most respects are not like other hospital-based physicians. Their field, however, has developed rapidly in the past 15 years because of the proven success of kidney transplants and the need to manage patients with serious kidney deficiencies over extended periods until a suitable transplant donor can be found. The kidney dialysis machine, together with the expertise provided by nephrologists and specially trained nurses, has been most successful in maintaining such "end stage" patients in relatively good health for several years. Currently there are well over 50,000 patients in the United States undergoing weekly dialysis treatment in end stage renal dialysis programs — and increasing at the rate of about 10,000 annually. In 1973, Medicare began providing coverage for all such patients, regardless of age; this has cost an average of $25,000 per patient annually.

The future of nephrologists as hospital-based physicians is somewhat unclear, for several reasons. First, their emergence as hospital-based physicians came when dialysis was considered to be most safely handled in a hospital. In recent years there has been a concerted effort by the federal government to regionalize and reduce the number of hospital-based end stage renal dialysis centers, and also to encourage the development of more economic "free standing" dialysis centers — free-standing, that is, from the costlier hospital environment. In addition, there has also been an effort to encourage more home dialysis services as an even less costly option to the free-standing outpatient units.

Compounding all this is the fact that a hospital that grants a group of nephrologists an exclusive franchise to operate an end stage renal dialysis unit may not be so clearly protected from a restraint of trade legal action as are pathologists and radiologists; I know of no specific successful or unsuccessful law suits on this matter but potential for such suits is very obvious. As a result, where nephrologists have a choice, they may choose to operate a free-standing rather than a hospital-based program to avoid this potential problem.

For those who might want to look it up, the case that decided the issue of hospital authority to grant exclusive rights to inhospital kidney dialysis units is *Lewin vs. St. Joseph Hospital of Orange, 82 Cal. App. 3d 368 (1978).*

Nephrologists are usually in a very strong bargaining position relative to their hospital relationships because the government has been favoring the free-standing option over the hospital-based units, and also because of a little trick most nephrologists know, but that few administrators learn about until it is too late, namely how to get through the Medicare hierarchy to obtain the "Medicare Provider Number" under the nephrologist's corporate name rather than the hospital's name. Once this has been accomplished, the hospital is virtually forced to offer an exclusive franchise arrangement (e.g. lease), lest the nephrologists take their unit to another institution or free-standing center.

In such a situation the hospital really is in no position to even suggest reasonable professional fees, much less regulate them. It should be pointed out that even though Medicare did specify a reasonable professional charge per procedure (e.g. $25), the total charge for dialysis was not so regulated, thereby giving nephrologists an incentive to operate their own programs. Hospitals that do have the provider number under their own name, do, of course, have this authority to regulate total charges and can use their position effectively because there is, in fact, a fair amount of competition among nephrology groups for such units now that the government has imposed tight regulations over the opening of any new units.

With Medicare spending roughly $1 billion annually on

such patients and with some technological advances in dialysis machines, it is likely that more hospital-based renal dialysis units will be phased out in favor of home dialysis and the role of hospital-based nephrologists will correspondingly become less significant.

3.6. Cardiologists, Neurologists, and Other Specialist Interpreters

The role of the hospital-based cardiologist is typically restricted to interpretation of electrocardiograms or the graphic tracings of heart activity determined from electrical impulses emanating from the heart. Basically the same applies to hospital-based neurologists when they are charged with the responsibility of interpreting electrically generated tracings of brain activity — the electroencephalograms. Similarly, the physiatrist or internist who interprets electromyleograms and the chest medicine internist or anesthesiologist who interprets pulmonary function tests, are hospital-based physicians under contract, formal or informal, to provide the hospital its specialty interpretations of these diagnostic tests.

In all cases these interpretations, like x--ray interpretations, become part of the medical record of each patient tested and the interpretations are available for the attending physician who requested the test in the first place. These interpretations are not considered "consultations" any more than an x-ray interpretation is a "consultation," though these specialists may subsequently be called in on consultation.

Given the growing complexity of some of these diagnostic, interpretive services and the changing technologies and technical staff required to perform such procedures, these hospital-based physicians are gradually assuming a broader role, beyond that of simple interpretations, and in some cases they provide medical supervision of the hospital ancillary department that renders these services. For example, a cardiologist may be assigned the role of "medical director" or "medical coordinator" for EKG Services, especially now that the Joint

Commission on Accreditation of Hospitals is suggesting mechanisms for internal auditing of these services. EKG departments now typically include more than simple EKG's, and may provide vector-cardiogram services, echocardiography services, stress testing (utilizing treadmills) and Houlter monitoring.

Cardiologists, neurologists and other internists who provide special interpretive services do not typically devote their full time to these roles (unlike radiologists, for example) but continue to carry on their private practice. The interpretations are usually just another source of income to complement their private practices. It is, therefore, not surprising that most such specialists do not consider themselves under a hospital-based physician contractual relationship with the hospital, and usually no formal contract terms exist. Also, their professional societies have not been deeply involved in defining their relationships with the hospital because even though most such specialists may provide these services to one or more hospitals, this is only a small part of their professional commitment.

Here are some issues relevant to these categories of hospital-based physicians:

1. Subspecialty boards in their area of expertise (cardiology, neurology, chest medicine), may be required before the hospital will grant them the restricted privilege of performing such interpretations.

Note: This frequently is a source of tension with cardiologists because most internists may feel their training qualifies them to interpret EKG's and may, therefore, resent being closed out of this professional involvement. As noninvasive cardiology gets more and more complicated (vectors and echocardiography, among others) most internists are beginning to recognize that their training is inadequate for this role. The role of the newly emerging subspecialists in chest medicine *vs.* anesthesiologists is another potential source of conflict in regard to pulmonary function testing and other inhalation therapy services.

2. Interpretive services are obviously volume related, *i.e.* the more interpretations required, the greater the work effort.

Typically, these physicians expect to be compensated for each interpretation rather than on salaried or a percentage of revenue basis.

Note: As with radiologists and other hospital-based physicians whose output is volume related, there is an incentive to keep this exclusive privilege restricted to the fewest specialists and, thereby, ensure the highest possible personal earnings. A typical hospital may have only three or four cardiologists on assigned rotation to do EKG interpretations even when there are six or seven equally well qualified cardiologists; sometimes they may agree to keep EKG interpretations among the senior cardiologists and allow only the more esoteric new noninvasive procedures such as vectorcardiograms, to be assigned to newer staff cardiologists.

3. Some potential conflicts may occur between the cardiologists and other specialists, such as the radiologists, over who should be responsible for interpreting such new diagnostic procedures as echocardiograms and phono cardiograms, and clear contractual terms will help avoid major problems in these areas. With the introduction of computerized axial tomographic head scanning, we can expect a dramatic reduction of EEG's and a shift of professional revenues from neurologists to radiologists.

4. Not surprisingly, cardiologists, chest medicine specialists and others may be reluctant to allow interpretive services to be provided by outside, on-line computer services even though such services may be more economical and more readily available on a 24 hour, seven day a week basis and may even offer more consistent interpretations. The computer services would obviously eliminate a source of income to which many of these specialists have become accustomed.

5. The hospital and its medical staff rather than the hospital-based cardiologist or neurologist generate the patient demand for interpretive services.

Note: With some such subspecialists, there is a possibility, however, of self-referral in a sense and a good contract negotiator will be aware of this. For example, an ambiguous, not-definitive EKG interpretation on a particular patient may leave the attending physicians almost no alternative but to request a cardiology consultation from the interpreter to clear up the issue. Unlike the radiologists, cardiologists (and other such subspecialists) can do consultations and bill directly for them.

6. Although there is no direct patient relationship (unless an interpretation generates an official consultation), some such specialists prefer to bill patients directly for their interpretive services, but, more typically, the hospital establishes a physician charge, bills the patient and reimburses the specialist.

3.7. Respiratory Medicine

1. Because respiratory care or inhalation therapy departments are developing rapidly in many hospitals (and also providing some extremely high net incomes), more and more specialists in chest and pulmonary medicine are getting involved as hospital-based physicians. There are more such board certified specialists available and the traditional involvement of anesthesiologists in these services is rapidly diminishing. These specialists do not yet have a strong professional society like the A.C.R. and C.A.P. but one may well be established soon.

2. More and more hospitals are seeking medical supervision of these departments and may be paying straight part-time salaries or other arrangements for this type of direction. With increasing numbers of seriously ill patients receiving ventilator care, such specialists must work with other medical staff members to ensure proper use of these services.

This raises the question of whether ventilator care is a consultation to the attending physician or whether it is a service provided to the patient by the hospital (through its contractual arrangement with the specialist). The question usually is a sticky issue because, on the one hand, the respiratory/pulmonary specialist may be reluctant to appear to be intruding into the clinical practice of the attending physician while on the other, the hospital may insist he must become involved with any patient on ventilator care (which involves the respiratory care therapists). Also, unless some restrictions are included in the contract, the respiratory/pulmonary specialist can take advantage of his special status by billing for ventilator consultation services even though the hospital may already be compensating him in some way for these services.

3. A common contractual arrangement suggested by many respiratory/pulmonary specialists is that they be given a percentage of revenue or fee-for-service on all pulmonary function and other related tests.

Note: The only caution to be observed here is that, given the relatively recent emergence of this specialty, it is quite possible that this may result in an unpredicted bonanza to the specialists and it may also encourage over-use of such diagnostic procedures as simple spirometry or nitrogen washouts.

3.8. Nuclear Physicians

As is true of emergency care and respiratory care, nuclear medicine is a rapidly developing area. Following are some of the key issues and concerns involved.

1. Nuclear physicians only recently obtained board certification status. Their professional society is becoming strong and taking a hard line in favor of the kind of direct billing arrangements favored by the American College of Radiologists.

2. In many respects the nuclear physicians are like radiologists and most of the points mentioned in the section on radiology are applicable here. They are dependent on the hospital's major capital commitments, its technical staff, and referrals of patients because they usually have no direct patient contacts except in therapeutic isotope procedures. Also, most nuclear physicians are radiologists by training and have been used to percentage of revenue or separate or direct billing arrangements. As can be expected, they are also used to high six-digit income levels.

3. Interesting, though, is the fact that nuclear medicine involves not only scanning procedures, but also *in vitro* "wet

lab" procedures such as radio-immuno assays, and to this extent nuclear physicians are somewhat like pathologists in their supervision of nuclear medicine laboratory procedures. In many hospitals, the pathology and radiology departments have had some hot contests over who should be responsible for nuclear medicine services — especially in those hospitals where neither the pathologists nor radiologists are on salaries, and hence this new source of revenue is worth fighting for.

A common solution is to split the department, *i.e.* the laboratory doing the "wet lab" procedures and radiology doing scanning procedures. Another common resolution has nuclear medicine as a subsection of the department of radiology although in a growing number of hospitals, nuclear medicine has attained a status that is independent of both departments.

Note: Given the fact that a portion of nuclear medicine services is similar to traditional laboratory services, the hospital negotiator should not permit compensation for such services to be on a volume or percentage of revenue basis. Also, obviously because of dissension and the desire of many nuclear physicians to get out from under both the radiology and pathology departments, the hospital may be in a good bargaining position to ensure, in return for this independence, some reasonable contract concessions. The hospital negotiator should, however, be aware of a common argument that the radiologists will put forth as to why this new specialty should not be separated from radiology, that is, they believe that radiologists should be allowed to participate actively in nuclear medicine services lest they be unable to develop skills and become expert in this area.

3.9. Unit/Department Medical Directors

With the growing need for quality control and medical audits, more and more hospitals are employing physicians to oversee the clinical activities of such units as intensive care and coronary care; the departments of respiratory care, physical therapy, EKG and EEG, and such specialty programs as alcohol treatment and mental health. Basically, this role is similar to that of medical administrators. The one critical difference, however, is that these unit and department medical directors are less involved with administration *per se* and more involved with monitoring clinical performance and compliance with established standards of medical care as rendered by staff physicians who use these departments or manage patients in these units. For example, the medical director of the coronary care unit may be responsible for ensuring that the necessary standards of cardiac care are not compromised by a physician who is not a cardiologist caring for his patient in this unit.

3.10. Medical Administrators

Medical administrators constitute a whole new breed of hospital-based physicians which is emerging as a consequence of several factors: Medicare regulations that require effective utilization review processes, the Bennett amendments to the 1972 Social Security Amendments that resulted in Professional Standards Review Organizations (P.S.R.O.s), the new directives of the Joint Commission on Accreditation of Hospitals, and, of course, the numerous judicial rulings that have defined the hospital's corporate responsibility (and liability) for ensuring the quality of care and practice of medicine within its institution.

The old concept that the hospital is simply a "physician's workshop" no longer is applicable, and so, too, is the notion that the medical staff is a free-standing self-governing body independent of the hospital and its governing body. Whereas elected officers of the medical staff used to represent the medical staff needs to the governing body and administration, more and more boards of trustees are appointing medical administrators, rather than relying on elected staff officers, to provide medical staff leadership and direction. The majority of hospitals in this country have not yet reached this point, but the corporate model is being adopted at an ever-increasing pace and more and more medical administrators will be appointed. These will include on a full-time or part-time basis: medical directors or "chiefs of staff," clinical department chairmen, directors of medical education, and special unit medical directors, among others.

Following are some special concerns and issues related to this group of physicians:

1. Typically, the method of compensation is not a complex issue. Straight salaries based on responsibilities or time commitment are accepted; more important is ensuring that other terms of the contract are clearly stated and accepted, especially the areas of responsibility, accountability and authority. This subject requires a book of its own, but the Catholic Hospital Association has developed some excellent guidelines.

2. Medical administrators suffer from a serious real or potential image problem with their fellow physicians. Historically, any physician who accepted a salaried administrative position was perceived by his counterparts in private practice as anything but a true physician. Typically, such positions were held by those in Veterans Administration and Armed Services hospitals, by socialists, ivory tower medical academicians and medical researchers, or by medical establishment dropouts or semiretired physicians put out to pasture. Virtually all the negative connotations that organized medicine applied to each of the hospital-based physicians discussed so far appear to be ascribed in the aggregate to appointed, salaried medical administrators. They tend to be viewed as pawns of administrators and boards and represent corporate (and, therefore, presumably bureaucratic) interference in the independent practice of medicine.

Note: It obviously requires an extremely competent and capable individual to fill this role without totally losing the credibility of the medical staff. It is, therefore, all the more important that his obligations and authorities are clearly delineated in a contract. Not surprisingly, medical administrators tend to have very short half-lives in this volatile environment.

3. Fortunately, medical administrators have a competent professional organization in the American Society of Medical Administrators which is helping establish the credibility and

identity of the professional medical administrator, although it will be many years before this role is fully accepted.

4. Medical administrators obviously have limited options to reassert their role as part of the medical community because they have no direct patient contacts, do not bill patients, or otherwise function in ways that apparently define a physician.

Note: For this reason, it is generally wise for management to allow its appointed medical administrators to continue to maintain small, limited private practices, although this can be fraught with competitive problems.

5. Part-time salaried medical administrators, such as clinical department chairmen, usually have the freedom to continue to participate in private clinical practices and, thereby, maintain some degree of credibility as a clinician.

Note: This can, however, have negative consequences in some cases. An appointed part-time chairman of pediatrics may quickly encounter some resistance from members of the department if it appears that the position, and its status, gives the appointee a competitive advantage, as it were.

HOSPITALS — THEIR POSITION

Following an expose by the *Detroit Free Press* in February 1973, Dr. Kenneth Williams, the former vice president of medical affairs of the Catholic Hospital Association, was asked why hospital administrators are reluctant to change specialist contracts that are obviously inequitable and "scandalous" as Dr. Williams had called them. His response: "They [administrators] don't have the guts to do it." Dr. Williams, a man of his convictions, had had the dubious privilege of personally testing what happens to an administrator with "guts." In 1968 he was medical administrator of a hospital in Detroit where the board of trustees apparently reneged at the twelfth hour on a mandate to administration that it renegotiate the radiologist's contract to put a ceiling on it. The radiologists balked and resigned and after the dust settled, three administrators were out of jobs, including Dr. Williams, the hospital's chief executive officer and an associate administrator.

Dr. Williams went on to point out that, in his opinion, hospital management and its trustees are responsible for perpetuating such contracts and that the beneficiaries of these arrangements — the hospital-based physicians — cannot be held responsible.

It is hard enough to understand why open ended contracts, with the predictable escalations of compensation, were ever allowed by hospital leaders, but some even more disturbing questions about the hospital's past position on this matter come to mind. If, according to one authority, at least $200 million is paid in excessive radiology, pathology and anesthesiology contracts annually, why was there no mention whatsoever in the "Voluntary Effort" guidelines [for cost containment] issued jointly by the Federation of American Hospitals and the American Hospital Association in 1977? Also, why have many hospitals failed to exercise their authority to regulate professional fees charged by these hospital-based physicians who were granted a monopoly arrangement in the hospital? So, too, in spite of the fact that from 5 percent to 9 percent of the hospital's operating costs go to hospital-based physicians as professional subsidies or payments, less than 50 percent of hospital-based physicians are operating under any kind of formal contract with their hospitals.

A simple television rental or laundry contract involving only $50,000 to $100,000 annually would typically involve a detailed contractual agreement between the hospital and the vendor, but a contract worth several hundred thousand dollars annually with a group of radiologists or pathologists apparently does not warrant such an effort. And even in those few salary contracts that have been developed, we sometimes find the "independent contractor" clause and clauses that allow such specialists some extraordinary administrative freedoms inconsistent with their real responsibilities.

Tradition is a hard factor to overcome. Again, we must look to the broader issue of the underlying confusion between hospitals and physicians and see how trustees and administrators have adapted. The implementation of the Medicare Development Act and several other important developments, including the Darling case, PL 93-641 (National Planning & Health Resources Act), PL 92-603 (the PSRO Act), rate review commissions and others, have dramatically changed the role of hospitals, their management and their governing boards. The current hospital-based physician contracts and agreements are really outdated remnants, long overdue for revision but ever and ever more difficult to revise because hospital-based physicians are understandably reluctant to give up $100,000 or so of their annual incomes. Today's administrators and trustees may be faced with an exponentially more difficult task of rectifying these arrangements than were those administrators and boards who sanctioned them 10 or 20 years ago. The responsibility to do so is no less great but the task is harder now.

To appreciate this dilemma fully, try to visualize the following hypothetical situation, which, unfortunately, may be close to the truth in some hospitals. Because of a percentage of revenue contract established eight years ago a group of hospital radiologists may now be earning average personal incomes of $200,000 each. Because of the nature of these revenue sharing contracts, just four years earlier they might have been earning only $80,000 or $90,000 each, but this income has escalated rapidly through no fault of the radiologists. The administrator may not have been worried about their compensation four years ago but suddenly it is now out of control. The board of trustees and its finance committee also should have been aware of what was happening, but perhaps they, too, like the administrator, may have thought they were dealing with a simple linear income growth curve rather than an income curve that compounds itself through volume increases plus rate increases — with no dampening effect created by competition — eventually yielding almost a 100 percent increase in four years. Nobody really planned it this way — not even the specialists involved.

Try to imagine what the administrator should do next. Does he advise the trustees that something both he and they sanctioned eight years ago is now totally out of hand? Whose fault is it? What can now be done about it? Can the administrator reasonably propose to the board that he renegotiate these contracts so the radiologists end up with more equitable annual incomes of, say, $100,000 or half of what they are earning at present? So preposterous would such a suggestion be that the administrator might earn himself a free room in his own hospital's psychiatric wing. Thus far, administrators may have been accused of being gutless and stupid, but they are not likely to want to add "crazy" to their list of attributes.

In a more moderate position, what realistically can he suggest to at least prevent this arrangement from getting even worse in the future? To suggest to the board that the administration would be willing to try to negotiate with his radiologists to freeze compensation at their current levels of $200,000 would require the board to sanction such salaries officially, something they would probably be very reluctant to do, especially if some local middle-income merchant or a housewife sits on the board and remembers that this is the same figure the President of the United States receives for his duties.

So what can be done? Likè an accountant who suddenly realizes he has taken an improper deduction on his company's tax return, the administrator may decide the consequences would be worse for him if he called this situation to the board's attention, and, therefore, decide to say nothing, hoping no one will notice. Of course, he knows it will be even worse next year and the year after but perhaps, he may reason, by then rate review commissions and third-party cost reimbursers may be controlling what hospital-based physicians can charge or be compensated for. Or perhaps, sometime in the future, the board may be willing to allow direct patient billing by hospital-based physicians and then neither the administrator nor the board will have to resolve this even more aggravated situation.

This is not the whole story, of course. There are other reasons administrators and governing boards may have allowed such contracts to begin with and then continued to allow them even when they got out of control.

Back in the mid-1950's, as has been mentioned, some hospital-based physicians were in a true seller's market and could command just about any contract terms they wanted. including the very favorable percentage of revenue arrangements. Then in 1966, amid all the confusion over Medicare, many of these physicians gained the support of their professional societies to force through contract changes that allowed them to bill directly on a fee-for-service basis — presumably consistent with a misinterpretation of the Medicare Act to make the direct billing arrangement appear, first, legally necessary, and then, ethically, the only acceptable option. At this point, many administrators probably felt they were fortunate to be able to retain their old percentage of revenue contracts with their specialists as the lesser of two evils.

Then by late 1966, when the legal and ethical arguments for direct billing by the professional societies did not hold up to a test, the American Medical Association encouraged its membership, on a nationwide basis, to support the hospital-based specialists, if necessary, in the contract negotiations with their hospitals. Because they had never had anything more than an ambiguous relationship with their medical staffs anyway, hospital governing boards may have been reluctant in the late 1960's to become embroiled in what might become an antagonistic relationship over these contracts with the staff-supported pathologists, radiologists and anesthesiologists. Boards of trustees do not like strife with the medical staff and, once again, bad hospital-based physician contracts may have seemed the lesser of two evils.

In the last 10 years, however, many things have occurred that have, or should have, changed the attitude of boards and administrators about their relationships with their medical staffs in general and their hospital-based physicians in particular. Important judicial decisions like the Darling *vs.* Charleston Community Memorial Hospital (Illinois, 1965), Moore *vs.* Trustees of Carson-Tahoe Hospital (Nevada, 1972), the Nork Case and others began to define the hospital's corporate responsibility for all aspects of care in the hospital, and it is now clearer than ever that the medical staff, like the hospital administrator, has an accountability to the governing body. The hospital is no longer a tripartite management shared equally with board, administration and medical staff.

As more boards have come to accept their corporate responsibility, the administrator is ceasing to be an "administrator" *per se* (the title of "hospital superintendent" is almost nonexistent) and more of the president/chief executive officer of the corporation. In this capacity he can be held more accountable to the board for all aspects of the hospital, including those that were formerly considered by the private medical staff as under their sole jurisdiction — including the arrangements the hospital has with its hospital-based specialists.

The dilemma of the Cecil County hospital administrator who probably got fired for granting a $433,000 pathologist contract as opposed to that of the Detroit hospital administrator who met a similar fate for trying to prevent such compensation may now be close to resolution, and so, too, may the situation most administrators have faced — where they knew they were in trouble for failing to do something but no one would tell them what they were supposed to do.

In this same period, several other judicial rulings have held the hospital responsible for the acts of its hospital-based physicians under the principle of *Respondeat Superior* — no matter what the financial arrangements between these physicians and the hospital, and regardless of whether the physician is called an "independent contractor" or not.

No doubt trustees have had to make a difficult trade-off in allowing such open ended contracts in their hospitals if only to avoid major conflict with their medical staffs as a whole. As any student of hospital administration knows, the hospital's real consumer is not the patient, but the physician who admits patients to it and uses its ancillary services. This is a reality administrators should be prepared to live with, but the board of trustees of a hospital has an additional critical factor to consider, namely, its responsibility to make sure the hospital performs in the best interest of the public it serves, and not just for the benefit of the physicians who use it or have contracts with it.

This responsibility includes not only ensuring the quality of care rendered in the institution but also ensuring reasonable costs and charges for services provided by it. Obviously a board that has allowed a special interest group of its staff (e.g. a pathologist) to earn exorbitant compensation is failing to fulfill its responsibility to the public it serves.

Another important consideration that affects the hospitals' position is that many of them are receiving more third-party payments, especially those in Sunbelt retirement areas where the majority of patients may be covered by Medicare and the inner city hospitals that serve large numbers of Medicaid patients. What this basically means is that there is relatively less financial incentive to contain or reduce costs in hospitals whose revenues are derived largely from cost reimbursement by third parties. Furthermore hospitals located in states that have implemented rate review commissions should prepare for efforts by their hospital-based physicians to get out of percentage of revenue contracts and change to direct billing arrangements.

Another aspect of the hospital's position that sometimes serves as a very subtle disincentive for administrators to turn away from revenue sharing contracts is that hospitals, too, may benefit by increased and excessive utilization of such ancillary services. This is particularly true for those hospitals that budget high profit margins in these ancillary departments, a situation that is no longer justified or warranted.

In evaluating their own positions, hospital negotiators should be aware that hospitals are basically monopsonistic **[i.e.** sole buyers of the service**]** and it is very easy to abuse this advantage for greater profits. Monopsonists have a powerful control over their resources (including professional staff and employees). Knowing that nurses and other specially trained health care professionals have relatively few opportunities to use their skills outside the hospital industry, hospitals may have a tendency to exploit these human resources when offering compensation or by making excessive work demands.

The hospital is the purchaser of very specialized resources and at most may only be competing with neighboring hospitals for their staffs. This possibility of monopsonistic exploitation can also apply to employed or contracted physician specialists, such as pathologists, radiologists, and emergency care physicians. These physicians are so dependent on hospitals that they basically have very few places to practice their specialty outside the hospital. If the hospital takes advantage of this it can offer very low compensation arrangements or restrict the number of resources (the number of hospital-based physicians) and, thereby, unfairly benefit by collecting greater profits.

This is what emergency care physicians and other hospital-based physicians fear most and hospitals that have exploited this advantage in the past will have a great deal of difficulty convincing their hospital-based physicians and their specialist societies that they can offer fair, competitive and equitable salaries. It is in this context that hospitals should view specialist societies as similar to unions to the extent that they both may be functioning to prevent exploitation of their membership.

In contrast to the position of hospital-based physicians, one of the most intriguing aspects of the hospital's position is that hospitals have no organized body or society that has promulgated its position, or at least not as definitively and as consistently as the American Medical Association, and the specialist organizations have. The American Hospital Association and other national, state and religious hospital associations have basically preferred to take no position and that with the exception of lease or concession arrangements, the A.H.A. favors basically any type of contract between hospitals and hospital-based physicians that is "best for them (the chief executive officer, the medical staff, the Board of Trustees, and the physician involved) and especially for the patients they serve." Unfortunately, the A.H.A. has not taken a position against percentage of revenue contracts, nor has it specifically taken a position against direct billing arrangements where the physician determines his own charges.

Unlike the A.M.A., the A.H.A. has not deemed it necessary, nor apparently worth while, to develop a section or division of its organization to assist hospitals in negotiating contracts with their physicians — even though these arrangements represent from 5 to 9 percent of the average hospital's operating costs. In its September 1976 *President's Newsletter,* the A.H.A. simply suggests that "Rather than rely on Congress to solve a difficult problem, hospital managers and boards should solve the problem themselves, and A.H.A.'s *Guidelines — Contractual Relationships Between Hospitals and Physicians* should be helpful where a problem does exist." Unless the 1976 data revealed in the Health Care Financing Administration's study issued by H.E.W. are grossly inaccurate, I believe that many hospital administrators and trustees throughout this country must improve their negotiating skills and could benefit by something more than a casual reading of the A.H.A. *Guidelines.* Alternatively, they should turn to outside expert help because obviously the managements and trustees of the nation's hospitals have not yet solved the problem by themselves and Congress may attempt to do so in the end. Fortunately, the American College of Hospital Administrators offers an excellent course on the process, art and technic of negotiating which, among other subjects, covers some aspects of hospital-based physicians negotiations.

It is curious, though, that back in 1966 the A.H.A. position was somewhat clearer and stronger, and following the implementation of the Medicare Act, the A.H.A. was quick to mobilize its efforts to stop an all-out direct billing campaign by the A.M.A. and the specialty societies. Now, however, hospitals cannot turn to the A.H.A. for support against percentage of revenue contracts, nor can it expect to find an A.H.A. position expressly opposed to direct billing arrangements. In my view there is no reason why the various national and state hospital associations should not take a stronger, more definitive position. Consider by contrast how unambiguous is the position taken by just one specialist society, the American Society of Anesthesiologists, in its 1963 *Statement of Policy:* Section VII "...Correspondingly, it is the duty and responsibility of each component society (*i.e.* state or county) to prevent encroachment of practices not in accordance with this statement of policy within its locality, to check the spread of such practices, to remedy existing conditions when necessary, and to recognize and correct violations."

Finally, as has been pointed out, negotiations between the hospital-based physician and the hospital is usually influenced by factors or parties external to the process. For physicians, this usually means the position of their professional societies, their colleagues at neighboring hospitals and even other physicians on their hospital's staff. For hospital management there are no such pressures but there is an even greater external influence — the public. Since the late 1960's, these remarkable arrangements and their financial consequences have become public knowledge and administrators and trustees will now have to take account of this factor in their negotiations.

BYSTANDERS TO THE NEGOTIATION PROCESS — THE PUBLIC

Usually a negotiation involves only two parties sitting across the table from each other, but in the complex situation of hospital-based physicians, a third party, long ignored, appears to have assumed a place in this process and is beginning to manifest its position where apparently both the hospital and the hospital-based physicians have failed to take proper account of their concerns.

This third party is a combination of the general public, consumers, legislators, intermediaries and the actual payers — all of whom are hearing more and more about escalating payments to physicians as the negotiation process to date has apparently failed. Perhaps more important, however, at least as far as the public is concerned, are the extraordinary incomes some individuals are now earning, which is something the public can easily grasp. These incomes must represent some serious administrative failures in the system that allows such contracts. After all, $400,000 paid to one individual is a bit hard for most people to identify with and they must wonder what any one person could do in a hospital to warrant this kind of payment.

Once this kind of information reaches the public, it becomes progressively more difficult for administrators and physicians to keep their maneuverings private. Both sides pay a high price in credibility with the public. Most notable of the public exposes of this problem were presented in the *Washington Post* in 1972, the *Detroit Free Press* in 1973, and the *Chicago Tribune* in 1977. Most of these exposes concluded with special editorials expressing the newspaper managements' concern over these arrangements. Subsequent letters to the editor made interesting reading and conveyed some of the underlying frustration and distrust many members of the public feel about hospitals and doctors.

Why was the public so outraged? And why does this issue keep exploding in the media again and again? There are probably several reasons. Obviously, there is the insatiable appetite of the mass media for sensational news, and some of these reported compensations are sensational. In addition, each such expose seems to quickly follow legislative hearings. Sen.

Philip Hart's Senate Anti-Trust hearings produced enough information for the *Washington Post* writers to sink their teeth into. Revisions or proposed revisions in the Medicare Act as it applies to hospitals and hospital-based physicians also caused a series of public hearings, and in 1977 Sen. Herman Talmadge's Senate Finance Health Subcommittee once again raised the question and also cost containment bills offered by Rep. Daniel Rostenkowski of Chicago and others in 1978 also brought the issue before the public. These were put into focus by the *Chicago Tribune, New York Times* and other newspapers throughout the country.

At the same time, however, there has been a notable disenchantment by the public as it perceives hospitals and physicians in general. Physicians participating in blatant Medicare and Medicaid frauds, hospitals exposed for excessive overbuilding of unneeded additions, and wildly escalating hospital and medical care costs have not helped the health field's image. In the mid-1970's we had some indication of its deteriorating credibility in the rash of malpractice suits filed against both hospitals and physicians.

Because most hospitals in this country operate under the over-all direction of boards of trustees, who presumably have a responsibility to the public they serve, one would have expected the governing board of hospitals throughout the country to be sensitive to the changing public sentiments and take action before being forced into it by unfavorable articles. Enactment of the National Planning Act (PL 93-641) made it clear that the federal government did not have confidence in the ability of hospitals and their boards to plan and coordinate their efforts in the best interests of the public.

"Certificate of Need" legislation is now mandatory in virtually all states and hospitals are no longer given the privilege of making major capital expenditures and adding beds without approval of areawide and state agencies. PL 93-641 also has specific membership requirements for consumer (nonprovider) participation in the health system agencies. Perhaps it was never formally said, but it certainly seems to imply that the government is no longer satisfied with the traditional role of boards of trustees' and their obligation to be sensitive to the public they serve. Creation of state rate review commissions also seems to have this implication and they, too, will provide a significant contribution by consumers. Several of the 1977 and 1978 cost containment bills also seemed to recognize that external incentives and regulations may be necessary to slow the escalation of hospital costs.

We now know from California's experiences with "Proposition 13" that the public is quite capable of mobilizing a consumer rebellion, should media pressures and other traditional legislative processes fail. We also now know that industry and labor which are ultimately responsible for a sizeable portion of the health insurance premiums paid by the public are prepared to manifest their interests. Medicare officials have long been vocal about their concerns because they have a 30 percent stake in cost reimbursement and hospitals are now under greater pressure than ever to prove they are capable of managing their own internal affairs effectively and efficiently.

Given all these third parties with vested interests in the outcome, it would certainly be a grave mistake for hospital administrators and trustees to continue to negotiate hospital-based physician contracts without demonstrating some concern for the public's probable reaction, and without recognizing the forces labor, industry and government can ultimately bring to bear to take this negotiation process entirely out of the hands of the hospitals and their specialists.

The warning in a *Chicago Tribune* editorial (Aug. 16, 1977) is worth repeating at this point. "If the hospitals and specialist's associations involved feel that there is an advantage for the public in their cozy arrangements, let them explain it. If not, they should work together — joined by insurance companies — to end it. There are enough causes of rising hospital costs which hospitals can't control; their sincerity will be enhanced if they do all they can to hold down the costs they can control."

PROSPECTS FOR A FINAL RESOLUTION

1. Letting Government Resolve the Problem

Is it really worth while for hospitals and their specialists to continue to attempt to negotiate new or revised contracts? After all, we know that the motivations and expectations of both primary parties, the hospital-based physicians and the hospital, are so complex and now so grossly divergent that some remarkable negotiating skills will be required to reconcile these differences.

We know, too, there are signs the public is clamoring for some swift resolution through its elected officials and the legislative process. It would certainly be easier for administrators and trustees to just have to implement a federal or state mandate that eliminated percentage of revenue and direct billing arrangements and required all hospital-based physicians to operate under reasonable salaries. It would not be perceived as the hospitals' fault if such drastic measures were mandated, and the hospitals could continue to enjoy good working relationships with these hospital-based physicians. Hospital medical staffs did not blame hospital administrators and trustees when the P.S.R.O. Act (PL 92-603) became a mandatory quality control program for all hospital staffs. Again, when some hospital administrators and trustees failed to coordinate their area-wide planning efforts voluntarily, and PL 93-641 (the National Health Facilities Planning Act) was imposed to reduce inter-hospital duplication of beds and major capital expenditures, few if any administrators and boards complained about their neighboring hospitals when they were no longer allowed to purchase the $500,000 computerized axial tomography unit they wanted in order to "beat the competitor."

With such governmental regulation there was no longer a need to negotiate with the medical staff over medical care audits and utilization review or with fellow hospital administrators as to who should provide what services and how many beds. This is now left to a third party to decide — a designated P.S.R.O. agency or an H.S.A. or a state planning agency. Thus, hospitals have fewer direct confrontations over such controversial issues.

Of course, they also have less freedom, and if hospital administrators, trustees, hospital-based physicians, and organized medicine allow the public, and eventually the government to intrude into the area of hospital-based physician contracts, the same consequences can be expected. In this sense, then, if nothing is done the prospects for resolution to this long-standing problem are clear, and then the focus of negotiation efforts will be after-the-fact and will involve an outside party, like a rate review commission.

What is really so bad about turning over some of the responsibility of the resolution of this problem to a third party? After all, a little loss of freedom is a small price to pay when well over $200 million is at stake (and growing almost exponentially each year). And third party mediators often play a valuable role when negotiations between two parties otherwise break down. When union leaders and management fail to reach a satisfactory solution, they may resort to mediation. If two parties have a basic distrust for each other but have a mutual trust in some third party, they may decide to turn the ultimate decision over to this third party. The problem, however, is that we are not talking about just a little loss of freedom, and such third parties as health systems agencies and rate review commissions are more than mediators.

Arbitration is another means of delegating the resolution of a problem to a third party, but in this case the first two parties irrevocably surrender full authority to this third party. The arbitrator has to be vested with the power of enforcement and both parties must accept his right to enforce. This is more like what will happen if regulatory agencies (or even advisory bodies to regulatory agencies) are created to resolve what hospital administrators and hospital-based physicians have failed to achieve through their own direct negotiations.

As any administrator who has ever had to face a rate review commission or a health systems agency knows by now, however, it is very difficult to bargain one's position when such agencies are not really impartial as an arbitrator is. They usually have a strong consumer orientation and do not always have a good grasp of the dynamics and complexities of the hospital and its staff. Thus, the prospect of compulsory arbitration by regulatory agencies may be less than a desirable resolution and the cure can sometimes be lethal when we allow someone else to resolve our problems.

2. Making the Problem Invisible

There is, however, a second option for resolution of this contract problem. If hospital administrators prefer not to renegotiate tough contracts to correct these abuses, but also do not want to give this authority to other agencies, they can simply support the current efforts of most medical societies in favor of direct billing. This would relieve the hospital from the responsibility for any abuses the hospital-based physicians might perpetuate because the financial contract would now be between the physician and the public.

From the hospital-based physician's point of view, this would also be an ideal solution, because once and for all his own personal income would be as confidential as that of other physicians. It would not be known to the hospital and, therefore, not subject to public scrutiny, which is what caused the issue to venture into the public domain in the first place. If only the I.R.S. and Swiss banks were aware of the \$200,000 to \$500,000 annual incomes some of these physicians were making, the public would not have known enough to become outraged. Therefore, one might argue that if we cannot do away with these abuses (short of government intrusion) we can at least make them invisible to the public eye, so perhaps all the public indignation will quietly subside.

This might appear to be a clear, quick solution, but it poses three major problems. First, it is probably too late. The public and its legislators already know what serious abuses have resulted and have no reason to assume this is a self-limiting problem that will resolve itself if it is allowed to go underground. Second, hospital administrators and trustees are in great disfavor because of this issue and, if for no other reason, the future credibility of hospital leadership in this country (as perceived by consumers, insurance carriers, and government) will rest on a highly visible, expeditious, and ultimately effective effort by administrators and trustees to correct their problem. Direct billing will not be perceived as a resolution.

Third, and most important, for all the reasons mentioned earlier, the direct billing arrangement represents a complete abdication of financial responsibility by hospital leadership in the very area where it is most obviously required. Wherever exclusive franchise or monopolistic arrangements are sanctioned there is a concomitant responsibility to ensure price regulation by the party that grants the monopoly, and rate setting cannot be delegated to the recipient of the exclusive franchise privilege.

What then is the solution? Whether we like it or not, the best solution is probably the most difficult one — renegotiating these contracts on an individual basis, hospital by hospital.

3. Renegotiating Toward a Resolution — A Consistent Approach

What makes this solution so difficult is that it not only may require some very tough negotiating behavior by administrators but it will certainly require an organized commitment to make these revisions in most hospitals throughout the country. If administrators and trustees can be made fully aware of the serious problems inherent in percentage of revenue contracts and direct billing arrangements, they will be more consistent in their rejection of these alternatives.

It is not easy to develop new contracts that are not compatible with local prevailing practices, and virtually impossible if neighboring hospital leaders continue to reinforce the precedent by sanctioning direct billing or percentage of revenue contracts. Unfortunately, local circumstances and prevailing practices may serve as the basis for perpetuating bad arrangements. In some areas of this country, fee-splitting may be a common practice among primary care physicians and surgeons, but the prevalance of this practice in a particular area does not make it right. So, too, the fact that some hospital-based physicians in certain areas earn personal incomes in excess of $300,000 does not make the contracts that allow these incomes correct, simply because that is the norm for the area. In a town with five hospitals, it only takes two or three totally irresponsible contractual arrangements with hospital-based physicians to cause a very undesirable areawide precedent, and the remaining hospitals will have virtually no choice with their specialists but to accept this precedent.

I must reiterate my belief that national, state and local hospital associations have to take an unambiguous position on such contracts. Virtually all specialty medical societies, including even the American Medical Association, have developed very clear, unequivocal positions, and the following section from the American Society of Anesthesiologists 1963 *State-*

ment of Policy is the kind of directive hospitals could use to develop and support their own negotiating position.

"Section VIII: This Statement of Policy is not the mere expression of an 'impractical' ideal. Each member of this society and each component society (state or county) must recognize and assume the responsibility of implementing it through the education of the public and of institutions, through publicity, through action in concert with hospital associations and local medical societies, and with the help of legal counsel, if necessary. The Society stands ready to advise and to assist the component societies in situations requiring more than local endeavor."

To the extent that hospital associations can help individual hospitals reconcile many of their inconsistent values vis-a-vis their relationships with their medical staffs, one more neurosis will be removed from this industry. After all, a neurotic simply has an inconsistent value system and lacks a way of reconciling it. With the help of hospital associations perhaps we can at least begin to identify these inconsistent values and instead of suppressing them, we can recognize them honestly as conflicts and, thereby, expose them for rational resolution.

In the following seven Proposals, the term "hospital associations" is used to mean national, state, regional and religious hospital associations, including: American Hospital Association, Federation of American Hospitals, Council of Community Hospitals, Protestant Hospital Association, and Catholic Hospital Association. The role of state hospital associations will be more important than ever before because rate review commissions are being implemented on a state-by-state basis and we can, therefore, expect the strong specialist pressures for direct billing to occur in those states that have or will soon have rate review commissions. The term "insurance carriers" is intended to mean Blue Cross/Blue Shield and private health insurance companies.

Proposal 1 — Hospital associations should thoroughly investigate hospital-based physician arrangements nationally and locally and if they validate the findings of previous studies (including the 1977 H.E.W. — H.C.F.A. Report), hospital associations should cease denying a problem exists, and begin to develop strategies to help resolve this problem.

Proposal 2 — Hospital associations should be more definitive in their recommendations and guidelines for hospitals; these should be no less specific than those of the various medical associations and specialty societies and should include at least the following:

A. A strong recommendation against percentage of revenue contracts as inefficient, counter-productive and contrary to reasonable hospital cost containment objectives.

B. A strong recommendation against direct fee-for-service billing arrangements as inefficient, counter-productive, inflationary and an inappropriate delegation of the authority for professional fee regulation under a franchise arrangement; and recommend instead that fee regulation be retained by the hospital to ensure no abuse and inflationary trends develop.

C. A strong recommendation against lease arrangements with hospital-based physicians both for the reasons previously stated and because of the loss of management control over their services by the hospital that would result.

D. Recommendations for specific types of contracts that are most appropriate for each major group of hospital-based physicians.

Proposal 3 — Insurance companies, state insurance departments, rate review commissions and the Social Security Administration should reinforce Proposal 2 and its specific recommendations and take a position similar to the position taken by the Pennsylvania Insurance Department.

Proposal 4 — Hospital associations should develop clear, definitive recommendations relative to the hospital's corporate responsibility for ensuring the quality of medical care (including the hospital-based physicians' services) in their institutions, similar to the guidelines established by the Catholic Hospital Association.

Proposal 5 — Hospital associations should develop comprehensive and effective educational programs for hospital administrators and trustees in at least the following areas:

A. Corporate responsibility for all services and care provided in their institutions.
B. Legal implications of several court rulings relative to corporate responsibility and the *Respondeat Superior* doctrine.
C. Cost reimbursement and prospective rate-setting implications to hospitals of salaries versus open-ended hospital-based physician contracts.
D. Economic and managerial implications of all types of prevalent contractual arrangements.

Note: The strategic importance of this education process by national, state and regional hospital associations should not be underestimated. Hospitals and their associations cannot, and should not, participate in collusive activities but a unified, consistent approach is needed.

As Gerard Nierenberg put it in his book, *The Art of Negotiating:* "Trade associations are faced with many problems, particularly in connection with anti-trust laws and price fixing. Price fixing by an association is illegal. There are, however, many things that trade associations can do legally in this field. For example, associations have initiated programs to educate their members in cost accounting procedures. The members are shown how to calculate the actual costs in their industry. They are then shown how to apply this data to their individual businesses by using uniform methods of accounting. After being thoroughly indoctrinated in this way, it is unlikely that any member will sell at prices below those that the association accountants suggest as a minimum."

Proposal 6—National hospital associations should develop consulting services and operating divisions on physician contract negotiations similar to services now offered by the American Medical Association and various medical specialty societies for their membership.

Proposal 7 — The joint F.A.H. — A.H.A. Voluntary Effort (VE) Program should include as one of its top priorities a cost containment effort relative to hospital-based physician contracts, and recommend that hospital cost containment committees include a careful analysis of all contracts with their hospital-based physicians for current and long range cost containment implications.

It is nothing short of ludicrous for national hospital associations to continue to ignore the cost containment implications of this $7.6 billion issue. This represents almost 5 percent of all U.S. health care (hospital, medical, dental, etc.), expenditures. Of the total, $4.6 billion relates to specialist incomes that are directly paid or reimbursed by hospitals, representing roughly 7 percent of hospital operating costs. The remaining $3 billion represents hospital-based physician incomes that the hospitals should control but currently do not because they have allowed almost 40 percent of such arrangements to function outside their control, *i.e.* by direct billing or lease arrangements.

If instead of cost containment recommendations for the conversion of 60 watt to 40 watt bulbs, the voluntary effort addressed itself to recommendations to convert open-ended specialist arrangements to contracts that are more effectively regulated by individual hospitals, some very substantial savings could result. A single 1 percent reduction of these payments, or even a 1 percent deceleration of the annual growth of these incomes, could yield a $78 million savings annually. What's more, such revised contracts could result in almost exponential savings in the years subsequent to their change and the $215 million excess annual specialist payments estimated by Dr. Sidney Wolfe of the Nader Health Group might be saved in less than three years.

Finally, the objectives cited do not discount the potential role of various hospital professional societies, such as the American College of Hospital Administrators, the Hospital Financial Management Association and the American Society of Hospital Attorneys. However, theirs' may only be a limited role until it is clearly decided who should be responsible for achieving the desired outcomes of the negotiations. Hospital attorneys can design contractual agreements to ensure that both parties fulfill their obligations, but they can do so only after the hospital defines its objectives and only if a formal, binding contract is mandated by the hospital's governing body.

Similarly, although the Hospital Financial Management Association offers courses for members on hospital-based physician contractual agreements, controllers or vice presidents for finance can only assist in devising arrangements that ensure reasonable compensation in relation to costs or other factors, but the objectives as well as the authority to negotiate toward these objectives rests with the hospital's governing board or its delegate, the chief executive officer. However, even the American College of Hospital Administrators may have a limited role in its efforts to educate the membership in regard to more effective, consistent negotiations with hospital-based physicians, because not all hospital governing boards give their administrators responsibility for developing the negotiating objectives or even the authority to carry out the negotiations.

The American College of Hospital Administrators offers a general course on negotiating technics for administrators but it was noted as recently as December 1977 that only slightly more than half the chief executives attending that seminar were responsible for negotiating with their hospital-based physicians. Consequently, less than 30 percent of the course material in this A.C.H.A. seminar relates to physician negotiations and as good as the program is, its focus is more on making the best of a bad situation (*i.e.* current, open ended contracts) than it is on negotiating toward the elimination or conversion of current contracts when such contracts are inequitable.

The important thing to keep in mind in all of this preparation is that support should be sought from every reasonable source. There really are not good guys and bad guys in the negotiation process. There are just different goals. When a physician is asked to review his income and, in effect, reduce it, this is a personal and, indeed, a painful request for reasons which we hope we have made clear by now.

As we also have noted, there are risks attendant to the review. A hospital could lose a specialist, as we shall see in our case histories. A hospital could lose its administrator — a not uncommon phenomenon. But the end result can be millions of dollars of savings to the hospital over a short span. If a position opens where a qualified physician can earn let us say, $90,000, because the physician who held the position left while earning let us say, $275,000, there is a huge saving. of course — assuming that a qualified physician can be attracted at $90,000 a year salary. My experience indicates this is often the case. If $90,000 a year won't do it, then $100,000 or $110,000 with fringe benefits will.

When the savings are potentially huge, the risks are likely to be large, too, especially if the board and the administrator are reluctant to face change and some unpleasantness. But the option, in many cases, is merely to substitute one form of unpleasantness — charges of ineffective management — for another form of unpleasantness that can save the community millions of dollars in the process. The choice, ultimately, rests with the board at the local level. But if enough boards at the local level do not make the right kind of choices, the choice may not reside with them much longer. We have seen this happen in the health care field many times, notably with regional planning, and we will see it happen again if we are not careful and responsive to all the implications of voluntary cost containment. We can't duck the thorny issues because they are thorny. Not if they have the potential to produce on a national basis hundreds of millions of dollars of savings.

NEGOTIATING PROCESS

1. Overview — Negotiations Between Precarious Partners

First, some assumptions to ponder: In the negotiating process, hospitals and their specialists may be both adversaries and allies over certain issues at different times or even at the same time; both parties cannot be assumed to be negotiating altruistically or in good faith; compromising or merely "reaching an agreement" is not synonymous with effective negotiating; the negotiation process may not be either a peaceful diplomatic process or a ruthlessly aggressive one; political maneuvering and Machiavellian moves are not a substitute for effective negotiation; and finally, like any other social process, effective negotiating behavior cannot be reduced to rules or axioms any more than the dynamics of human interrelationships can be defined by a scientific method.

For several reasons the negotiation process between hospitals and their physicians is not amenable to traditional negotiating theory and techniques. Most important, perhaps, is the fact that theirs is a uniquely complex relationship to begin with. In more traditional negotiations the hospital may only have a limited relationship with another party, as for example when it negotiates with an architect and a contractor for the design and construction of a $10 million addition, or with a manufacturer for the purchase of a major piece of equipment. These relationships are limited in scope and time while the one between hospitals and their specialists may be so close that it sometimes borders on a personal contract for services. Also, unlike the negotiation process between the hospital and a labor union that represents its employees, negotiations with hospital-based physicians involve dealing with professional persons whose motivations cannot be reduced to simple wage and fringe benefit packages and working conditions but are more complex and less definable and may include such factors as professional freedom, privilege and prestige.

The relations between hospitals and their specialists have

become even more complex in the past several years as third parties, including the media, consumer activists, legislative and regulatory agencies, have begun to demonstrate a vested interest, and in some cases exert a direct influence. This, in turn, makes the negotiation process more complex and may even totally alter it. Not only must the results of these privately negotiated arrangements be beyond public censure if they are exposed but, more importantly, when third parties have the authority to influence or control outcomes of the two negotiating parties (the hospital and its specialists) the whole negotiation process may shift dramatically from one of pure competition and conflict to one of pure cooperation and coordination between the hospital and its specialist.

In game theory this is not unlike converting a game of poker or chess into a game of charades, the former requiring competitive behavior between the two parties, while the latter requires a concerted effort to work together to win over, or at least appease, a third party. In its most dramatic form this latter situation would arise in states that empower their hospital rate review commissions with the authority to regulate both hospital charges and charges made by hospital-based physicians.

At the other extreme, in a totally unregulated environment, hospitals and their specialists may be more akin to chess players (who may be only indirectly and remotely influenced by other parties) and in game theory theirs would be called a "zero sum game" because by and large they are economic adversaries rather than partners and, as such, what one loses the other gains.

Somewhere between these extremes we are likely to find most hospitals and their hospital-based physicians, that is, not purely competitive nor purely cooperative. For this reason perhaps the only adequate way to describe their negotiation relationship is that of "precarious partners," or "incomplete antagonism," terms Thomas Schelling used in *The Strategy of Conflict* to define the relationship between potential friends who are also potential enemies. In the hospital setting, pathologists, radiologists, and other hospital-based physicians may become economic competitors and adversaries of the hospital, especially when their incomes escalate into six digits, at the time hospitals are finding its progressively more difficult to generate other sources of new revenue to offset increasing costs elsewhere in the system.

However, aside from the economic relationship, these hospital-based physicians continue to be important allies or "friends" of the hospital in providing critical diagnostic and support services. In this precarious partnership both parties will lose if they can't find some way of cooperating, but neither party can afford to acquiesce to all the needs or wants of the other — even for the sake of peace.

Under this definition of precarious partnerships as the basis for negotiation between hospitals and hospital-based physicians, the negotiation process may be less simple and straight forward than is usually suggested in traditional negotiating theory. For example, this process may require us to begin to think in terms of the use of gambits rather than clear-cut concessions even though both represent giving up something. Gambits are deliberate but subtle sacrifices (a pawn in chess, for example) to gain an advantage in one's position, while concessions are overt trade-offs, the purpose of which is known to both parties. So, too, in this process we may have to recognize the importance and value of threats in effective negotiations and not equate these threats with antagonistic, provocative behavior or false bluffing. Threats have strategic value because they can, if properly manifested, affect the expectations of the other party about our behavior and, thereby, modify the outcome of negotiations. Warnings, by contrast, represent simple, straight-forward information from one party to another and although this may be important it has very little strategic value.

Also contrary to our usual understanding of negotiation, we should recognize that the process itself may have to be tough, unrelenting and impersonal. This may be especially difficult for the hospital administrator who has had a long-standing personal relationship with a chief radiologist or anesthesiologist, but by the very nature of the process it has to be impersonal from the hospital's point of view. This, incidentally, does not mean that subsequent relations between the administrator and the physician have to be cold anymore than a disagreement between a husband and wife or a boss and a subordinate would doom these relationships forever.

Negotiation is a skillful, impersonal process and requires the kind of objective commitment that a surgeon applies to a difficult surgical procedure: that is, it requires his best skill and judgment, no matter who the patient is or what the surgeon thinks of him. There are, in fact, very real strategic advantages to be gained by the physicians to prevent this process from becoming impersonal, and the hospital negotiator's task may be even more difficult in this respect. With his personal income and professional freedoms at stake, we cannot assume that the hospital-based physician is altruistic or otherwise free of all selfish motives or that what he wants is best for the hospital any more than the physician can assume that the hospital is totally altruistic.

Going one step further, effective negotiations may require the hospital negotiator to enter this process with a healthy distrust of the other party. This may sound like the antithesis of good, open negotiating behavior, but as a matter of fact, there would be no need at all for negotiations or renegotiations if there was not some potential for conflicting motives and values. When this potential exists we cannot take for granted trust and perfect harmony between the parties.

This negotiating process between hospitals and their specialists may involve compromises, but compromises *per se* are only a very small part of effective negotiations. Hospital administrators are inclined to compromise, especially in their relation with physicians, but compromising is not a substitute for effective negotiating skills and strategies. If a hospital-based physician's demands are outrageous to begin with, going half way with him only makes the administrator's compromise half as ridiculous as it might have been. On occasion, boards of trustees may inadvertently sanction this compromise-oriented attitude of their executive officers by reinforcing (and even rewarding) them more on the basis of their ability to reach agreements than on how favorable the terms of the agreement are for the hospital and its patients.

We must be careful not to assume that all situations are negotiable; nor should we try to make all situations negotiable simply by focusing on the simplest and most negotiable parts of a situation. A physician who is not prepared under any circumstances to phase out his lucrative $300,000 per year percentage of revenue contract should not be offered the opportunity to negotiate down from, say 35 percent of gross to 32 percent as a concession. This is only a short-term solution and even though it may represent an agreement, it certainly is not favorable to the hospital for any more than a year or two, given the inherent escalating nature of these arrangements. It is not true that in successful negotiations everyone wins. A negotiation effort that results in the resignation of an unreasonable specialist may be more desirable than simply negotiating for an agreement over minor issues and with inconsequential concessions.

Although effective negotiations may involve political savvy and diplomatic skills, the negotiation process between hospitals and hospital-based physicians is not synonymous with, or a substitute for, political wheeling and dealing or diplomacy. A hospital negotiator may find it impossible to remain the diplomat in a tough negotiation process in which subtle or overt threatening behavior is employed against him or drastic concessions are required as, for example, when a $400,000 open ended income arrangement has to be brought back to a fixed income plan in the middle $100,000 range. On the other hand, an administrator may find it excessively risky to play shuttle politics when the issues are extremely sensitive.

Negotiation is not governed by any clear-cut rules or regulations. It is a fluid, dynamic process that depends more on the situation, the circumstances and the individuals involved, and it can quickly become extremely complex. It is basically concerned with the individual expectations and needs of both parties, but each party's behavior in the actual negotiation can modify the expectations (and then the subsequent behavior) of the other party and *vice versa* — a back and forth process that in mathematics can probably only be approximated by an infinite regression curve.

The negotiating parties develop their own "rules of the game" as they get deeper and deeper into this process of trying to influence each other's expectations by trying to anticipate how their behavior will be perceived by each move or statement they make. Royce Coffin, author of *Negotiation, A Manual for Winners* put it this way: "In most negotiations, success or failure is determined more by the actions, inactions, habits, idiosyncrasies, blunders, insights and clever strategic moves of the individuals involved than by the terms of the agreement or other formal elements of the proposed transaction."

We should look upon negotiation as an ongoing, perpetual process that begins long before the first formal meeting between two parties and does not end with the signing of a contract. Prenegotiation strategy is as important as the actual one-on-one negotiation meeting that brings all the strategies and tactics into use.

In this prenegotiation phase the objectives are established first, followed by the board's commitment to them and the subsequent development of a plan or broad strategy to achieve these objectives. A simple error of delegation or failure to appreciate the importance of sustaining commitment can make subsequent strategies and maneuvers futile. It is also during the prenegotiation phase that the hospital negotiator can inconspicuously begin to enhance his bargaining power. For example, he may have to disengage himself gradually from any personal relationship he may have had with the hospital-based physician, so his subsequent bargaining behavior and commitment can be more objective and, if necessary, impersonal.

Although the negotiation process may appear to end with a formal written contract, it usually continues in one form or another; the only exception to this may be when the end product is an agreement to allow the specialist to bill patients directly, which, in fact, is really an agreement to cease any future negotiations between the hospital and the specialists.

In other cases, however, the signed contract can only fix some of the rules of the relationship between the two parties and, thereby, focus future negotiations into this confined range of expectations.

A clause in the contract, for example, that grants the chief radiologist the authority to recommend specific supply and capital purchases for the department, by its very nature, leaves room for negotiation between the two parties. Even though management may have the final authority in these matters, it will be wise not to manifest its authority without very good reasons. Although it may be possible to save $50,000 annually by the purchase of foreign-made x-ray film, this will become a negotiable issue rather than a mandate because clinical judgments by the radiologists may be compromised by such a decision.

2. Formulating and Validating the Hospital's Position

Before the hospital negotiator can develop a strategy for negotiating or renegotiating hospital-based physician contracts, he obviously has to define his own position and the desired outcome. As has been noted, there have been several developments in the past 15 years that have helped delineate a new and clearer role for hospitals in their relationships with physicians in general and with hospital-based physicians in particular and these must somehow be incorporated into the hospital's bargaining position.

Similarly, owing to the economic implications in the relationship between hospitals and their physician franchisees, the hospital can no longer take a neutral position between these providers and the patient. In effect, the hospital's position must cease being like that of casino or racetrack management that gets a "housetake" or percentage of the "bite" for handling the transactions between the public and these specialists. The hospital has to have ultimate authority to regulate these professional fees as well as to ensure both the adequacy and availability of the services provided.

Attorney James Ludlam of the Los Angeles firm of Musick, Peeler and Garrett briefly summarized three simple objectives the hospitals should seek in their negotiations with these specialists which were included in Appendix C of the 1976 American Hospital Association's *Guidelines on Contractual Relationships between Hospitals and Physicians*:

1. Fair and reasonable cost to patients
2. Assurance of quality
3. Mutual confidence within the triangle of specialist, medical staff, and administration

Although this is an adequate summary of the hospital's basic position, some further clarification and additional objectives may be worth considering in formulating the final position.

First, when we define as one of our objectives the assurance of fair and reasonable costs to patients we should consider not just the professional fee structure but other factors under the control of hospital-based physicians that might directly or indirectly increase the cost of patient care. For example, as has been noted, certain contractual arrangements may inadvertently reward pathologists (or radiologists) for operating inefficiencies in their departments as is the case when the contract allows compensation on the basis of a percentage of gross revenues or charges generated by the department.

To cover the costs of these inefficiencies the hospital will have to raise its laboratory (or x-ray) charges and the hospital-based physicians automatically benefit because their earnings relate directly to the revenue coming into the department. The very nature of some of these contracts could conceivably give the radiologist, pathologist or other hospital-based specialist an incentive to encourage the purchase of non-cost-effective equipment or other resources to render services that might be more efficiently provided by private reference laboratories or neighboring hospitals.

In addition, one of the most serious causes of escalating health care costs is excessive or unnecessary utilization of services, and most current contractual relationships between hospitals and hospital-based physicians provide these specialists with a personal financial incentive to encourage excessive over-ordering of diagnostic services. Whether the specialist is compensated on a fee-for-service or percentage of revenue basis, the more tests he orders, the greater his income. Obviously, this could lead to abuses in some cases.

It is not easy to determine the real cost of these counter-incentives to efficiency and productivity but it is interesting to note that apparently one 260 bed hospital satisfied its state rate review commission that $140,000 could be saved annually by eliminating them in their radiology contracts. In late 1978 the Connecticut Commission on Hospitals and Health Care approved the request by this hospital to put its four radiologists on salary and, thereby, eliminate a previous fee-for-service arrangement on the basis that substantial savings would accrue to patients by the reduction of unnecessary x-rays. For these reasons, then, the hospital's objective should be the design and implementation of only contractual arrangements that do not encourage escalation of hospital costs which ultimately become unreasonable costs to be borne by the public. In a broader sense, the hospital's position in these types of contract negotiations should be based on a clear cost containment objective.

Obviously, if the hospital is to assure fair and reasonable costs to patients in relation to hospital-based physicians, the hospital also must ensure that the professional charges for these services are reasonable. The hospital should take the position in these negotiations that it has the authority to regulate these professional fees so it can ensure that both current and future fee structures are reasonable. The hospital does have this authority, and should wield it on the basis that it is granting an exclusive franchise to these specialists and, therefore, has the obligation of regulating such fees in the absence of competitive, free market conditions that would help prevent unfair pricing. A secondary but less critical reason hospitals have the authority to regulate these professional fees is that the hospital provides all the necessary capital, supplies and manpower to make it possible for the specialists to perform their functions and the hospital shares with the specialist responsibility and legal liability for the services provided. For these and many other reasons the hospital's position should not be favorable to direct billing by its specialists or any other arrangements that might cause the hospital to lose its authority to regulate the charges or even its authority to ensure periodic review and renegotiation of the fees.

Hospitals may have difficulty in their attempts to establish a position relative to reasonable professional charges. For example, should "reasonable" be defined in relation to what other hospital-based physicians charge for their services? The answer might be yes, if neighboring hospitals have regulated their fee structures, but not if exorbitant professional price-setting practices have been sanctioned by those hospitals.

Again, it may be difficult to determine what is a reasonable professional fee for one procedure in relation to another. For example, we might expect that a lumbar spinal x-ray interpretation would entail a higher professional fee than a chest x-ray interpretation because the former requires more time and skill, but no such pattern may be evident when we look at our radiologist's pricing structure or even the pricing structures of neighboring hospital radiologists. What we might find is that certain high volume procedures are priced high for obvious reasons and also certain procedures might be priced relatively low to attract outpatient referrals for these services.

We may need to look at something more than prevalent fees in the local areas as a basis for determining reasonable professional charge structures. It is for this reason that the hospital should consider using standardized relative value scales so it can ensure that its professional fees are at least consistent with professional effort and skills. Until a 1979 N.Y. court ruling, the U.S. Justice Department prohibited professional societies from promulgating their own relative value indexes, presumably (but incorrectly) on the basis that this represents price fixing; hospitals were not prohibited from using or developing their own relative value indexes, although acting in concert, hospitals could be accused of limiting the market artificially.

In the special case of the pathologist's professional fees there is virtually no relation between the professional skills and efforts of pathologists and the vast majority of tests performed by the laboratory. Aside from anatomical pathological procedures which rarely represent more than 10 percent of a laboratory's output, the primary role of pathologists is supervisory and there is really no point in trying to determine what is a reasonable professional fee for a CBC, a urinalysis, and the other procedures performed by the clinical laboratory.

In attempting to determine what are reasonable costs and charges for other hospital-based physician services we might be tempted to turn the question around and ask what would be a reasonable level of compensation for these specialists and then develop a fee structure that results in such income levels. There are a few problems with this approach and the hospital negotiator is cautioned not to take too explicit a position as to what he thinks an appropriate income level should be for these specialists, unless he can offer some objective basis for his position.

Strategically it is very difficult to make quantitative commitments seem real and credible, — *i.e.* the administrator's so-called commitment to offer $80,000 or $90,000 is virtually an invitation to a challenge. Qualitative commitments on specific principles (e.g. no open ended contracts) can withstand challenges and the commitment can usually remain intact. Obviously, at the extremes of $300,000 or $400,000 annual incomes, the hospital negotiator can take a strong position, but on what basis can he decide whether the professional services of a radiologist or emergency care physician are worth $75,000 or $100,000 or $115,000?

Even if we refer to national or regional income data on these specialists as a benchmark we find their average incomes significantly higher than those of non-hospital-based physicians, which may be more a consequence and indication of poorly negotiated, open ended extant contracts than a reflection of their true economic value in the health care system. For example, *Medical Economics'* continuing survey of physician earnings revealed that in 1977 the average net earnings of all U.S. physicians on a nationwide sample basis was $65,430; general surgeons averaged $68,720, urologists $80,770 and so on. By and large, free market and normal supply and demand conditions have determined these physicians' economic value and consequently their compensation. Similar competitive conditions have not applied to hospital-based physicians because of their unique arrangements with hospitals and thus their significantly higher average incomes do not necessarily mean they are more highly qualified physicians or that their work efforts and contributions are greater than those of other physicians.

How, then, can the hospital develop a position relative to reasonable professional charges and reasonable compensation levels for these specialists? There may be no simple answer but the following suggestions are offered for consideration.

On one hand, the hospital can specify that its professional charges should at least be in the lower half of the range of similar charges for its service area. At the same time, the hospital could also use H.E.W.'s Health Care Financing Administration's *Study of Reimbursement and Practice Arrangements of Provider-Based Physicians* to establish a target income level for the negotiations. For example, this study revealed that the average income of all radiologists was $103,200 while radiologists on salaries earned an average of $52,600 annually. The former figure probably represents an inflated level of compensation resulting from open ended fee-for-service and revenue sharing contracts while the latter figure may be unacceptably low for the negotiations.

The hospital might take as its starting position $78,000, which represents the average of these two extremes, and then either offer this as a straight salary or revise the professional radiologist fees to ensure that this level of income is earned. In light of the comments made earlier about the futility of trying to make a quantitative commitment seem credible and not negotiable, the negotiator would be much wiser to offer such a figure and not pretend to be committed to it. *[Note:* These figures are based on 1975 survey data and should be inflated at the cost of living rate over the past three or four years to make them current; also, the HCFA study provides regional figures which may be more useful and it also provides similar compensation figures for pathologists, cardiologists, anesthesiologists and emergency care physicians*]*.

In regard to Mr. Ludlam's second recommended position for the hospital, *i.e.* quality assurance, the hospital's position must be unequivocal in ensuring that adequate quality control mechanisms are established by the chiefs of these specialty services, including the quality of care rendered by emergency physicians, anesthesiologists, physiatrists, as well as the quality and consistency of interpretations performed by cardiologists, radiologists, nuclear physicians, pathologists, EEG interpreters, pulmonary function interpreters and others. Medical directors of specialty units such as intensive care, coronary care, and alcohol rehabilitation and clinical department chairmen should be charged with the responsibility of monitoring the quality of clinical care rendered by staff physicians who use these specialty units and members of their department.

When we speak of quality of care it is important that we not confuse the proper role of the hospital with that of the physicians to whom it delegates this quality control function. A lay board of trustees and a lay chief executive officer cannot be expected to directly determine (and control) what constitutes good clinical care and good medical judgment. Rather the hospital manifests its corporate responsibility in this respect by ensuring that effective quality control systems are established and it can best accomplish this by clearly defining these obligations in the contracts with its hospital-based physicians. The hospital also retains the ultimate responsibility for ensuring the quality of the technical and nursing services performed in these departments and units, even though it [the hospital], may choose to delegate fulfillment of this function to its appointed specialist or to the chief technologist, chief therapist, head nurse or clinical care specialists assigned to these departments and units. The critical point is that the hospital, not the hospital-based physician, retains the ultimate responsibility for all aspects of the quality of these services.

Mr. Ludlam's third recommended position for the hospital suggests the need for ensuring mutual confidence between the hospital-based physician, the medical staff and hospital administration, as an end product of those negotiations. Even though it has been suggested that in actual negotiations a healthy distrust by both parties may be useful, the final result of effective contract negotiations will, in fact, minimize the area of distrust between the two parties as they carry out their roles.

The terms of a formal contract will define more explicitly what each other's mutual expectations of performance are and will leave less to guesswork and potential confrontations. Therefore, it is strongly recommended that the hospital stipulate that there must be a formal contract of service. In addition, with the possible exception of specific compensation details, the terms of these contracts between the hospital and their hospital-based physicians should be known, understood and consistent with the diagnostic and therapeutic needs expressed by the medical staff, preferably through a review by its medical executive committee. Even though the medical staff should not have the ultimate authority to approve or disapprove of such contracts or any of their terms, they should have a right to make recommendations relative to the range, availability and quality of services the hospital-based physician will be expected by the hospital to provide.

Going somewhat beyond Mr. Ludlam's recommendation that encourages mutual confidence among the specialist, the medical staff and hospital administration, the hospital's position in these negotiations should recognize the importance of other parties, and the hospital negotiator would be well advised to heed the advice of David Hitt in his article, "Contractual Arrangements Between Physicians and Hospitals — An Administrator's View" (published in *The Hospital Medical Staff,* February 1977): "The rising tide of criticism concerning the cost of contractual services . . . places upon the contracting physicians and the hospital the heavy burden of not only achieving a privately acceptable arrangement but also ensuring that the terms of the contract, if publicized, will not be embarrassing to the physician or the institution."

Over and above Mr. Ludlam's three basic recommended objectives for the hospital in formulating its position, some others should be considered. The hospital should make it clear that it, the hospital rather than the physician, is providing any service rendered to patients as a hospital service and the hospital is corporately responsible and liable for all services provided by the institution. As such, the hospital is, therefore, ultimately responsible for all personnel, purchasing, financial and other administrative functions of the department. The hospital-based physician should not be entitled to hire his own employees or purchase his own equipment and supplies for use in the department. This position clearly precludes lease arrangements between the hospital and the specialist because under these circumstances the hospital cannot adequately manifest its responsibility to manage and control these hospital services —even though the physician is also liable for professional errors.

As a corollary to Mr. Ludlam's quality of care point, the hospital should also retain the authority to determine what level of professional staffing and what qualifications are required to ensure adequate quality and availability of services, especially under those contractual arrangements that leave the specialists a financial incentive to keep their professional staffing minimal. On the other hand, under salaried or fixed compensation arrangements the hospital has the obligation to ensure adequate professional staffing as recommended by the chief of the specialty service.

Finally, the hospital should clearly articulate a position that prohibits conflicts of interest by its hospital-based physicians and, more specifically, this might include provisions that do not allow other employment without prior hospital approval. It should also prohibit private, direct-billing consultations or self-referrals and restrict participation in private practices that could encourage referrals in competition with the hospital.

In summary, the hospital's negotiating position could reasonably include the following nine objectives:

1. Cost effective compensation arrangements which are consistent with aggressive hospital cost containment efforts and which by the terms of the contract do not encourage operational inefficiencies, counter-productive allocation of resources, or excessive utilization of diagnostic and therapeutic services. This objective would preclude virtually all revenue sharing, lease and direct billing compensation arrangements.

2. Compensation arrangements that are not open ended or otherwise capable of rapidly escalating out of control; this objective would preclude all current percentage of revenue plans except possibly those with fixed upper limits.

3. Reasonable and fair professional charge structures that can be assured by the hospital's ultimate authority to regulate all hospital-based physicians' professional fees.

4. Compensation arrangements which are not only fair and reasonable for both parties but which also will be perceived as fair by the public and other third parties.

5. Recognition and acceptance of the principle that the hospital has the ultimate authority to ensure that adequate quality control mechanisms exist for both the medical and nursing or technical support services rendered in those departments.

6. Ultimate authority by the hospital to determine the required level of professional staffing, in relation to the volume of services rendered by the department, and the qualifications of specialists to carry out these services.

7. Recognition that all services provided by hospital-based physicians are hospital services and can no longer legitimately be considered as services provided by independent contractors; that the hospital has both a corporate responsibility and a legal obligation under the principle of *Respondeat Superior* to control these hospital services and be directly responsible for all personnel, purchasing, financial and administrative functions of these departments.

8. Contract terms that prohibit or eliminate conflicts of interest by the hospital-based physicians.

9. A formal contractual arrangement between the hospital and its hospital-based physicians that includes such issues as the range, availability and quality of the services to be provided which should be consistent with both the medical staff requirements and the hospital's capability and resources to provide these services.

The points raised here are not intended to represent all aspects of the hospital's desired negotiating position, nor is it expected that all these objectives should be resolved once and for all in the contract. The hospital's position might include mandatory malpractice/liability insurance coverage with specific minimums, responsibility for bad debts, termination clauses, and several other issues. It should also be pointed out that some of these objectives will, in fact, require constant review and renegotiation and the hospital's position may be simply to ensure that continued negotiations will occur around one issue or another.

For example, if the hospital takes no position on its ultimate authority to ensure adequate professional staffing in relation to the volume of services rendered, it may be very difficult later to come back and demand the hiring of an additional specialist, especially if this results in a reduction of personal income to the other specialists. If, however, the hospital has clearly established this position and authority, it is much easier to ensure an annual review of volume of services and negotiate staffing additions, if warranted, in relation to increased departmental activity. Also, a decision to allow a specialist to bill patients directly is basically a decision to give up the right to ensure future negotiation over professional rates.

2.1. Validating the Hospital's Position

After the basic negotiating objectives have been established but prior to the actual negotiations, the hospital administrator should gather as much information as possible to validate his position. In this process he might find that one objective or another may not be so critical or may be difficult to support. To the extent that the hospital administrator can objectively support his position, he not only increases the likelihood of full understanding and commitment of the board of trustees to this position, but potentially enhances his own bargaining power during the actual negotiations.

An internal evaluation and an areawide survey of professional charges, compensation arrangements, compensation levels and other contractual terms are basic requirements for validating the hospital's position. The information gathered may confirm undesirable trends or comparatively unreasonable charges and compensation levels. Such a survey does have some limitations, however, because an arrangement or practice may not necessarily be acceptable just because it is prevalent.

The following internal evaluation check list may serve as a rough guide to some of the key issues that should be answered to validate the aforementioned nine objectives.

1. In regard to Objective 1, cost containment, does the hospital have a relatively higher diagnostic service utilization

rate (per admission or per length of stay or other criteria) than do other hospitals of similar size and type, based on regional Blue Cross/Blue Shield comparative data or Hospital Administrative Services (H.A.S.) data? *Note:* some Blue Cross plans have very sophisticated reporting systems that can provide comparisons of such things as the average total x-ray charge per admission or per admission diagnosis (e.g. appendicitis) so a hospital can determine if its aggregate x-ray charges or x-ray utilization rates are excessively high compared with those of other hospitals.

2. What are the negative consequences of the current open-ended contractual arrangement in terms of rapid escalation of compensation or compensation increases that exceed cost of living increases? (This relates to Objective 2.)

An historical analysis of the specialist's compensation (on a full-time equivalent basis over the past five years) may reveal escalation in excess of the cost of living for the same period, due to either increased hospital charges and increased volume of services in this department, or both. A detailed study of the hospital's rate increases for the x-ray department over this five-year period may reveal, for example, an annual rate increase of 10 percent (or slightly more than 50 percent in five years). In addition, a five year study of volume increases in this department may reveal, as an example, a 5 percent growth per year. If both these factors are combined the department's revenue will have increased by almost 100 percent in this period. By comparing these figures with the specialist's compensation in the aggregate and per full-time equivalent for this same period, it will be possible to determine if their current contract allows them to share automatically in this escalation. If the average earnings per full-time equivalent radiologist was $50,000 five years ago and is now $100,000, obviously their income has escalated as a function of both these two factors, with the same number of radiologists handling 50 percent more procedures.

To determine the real cost of these open-ended contracts we could develop a model assuming that the $50,000 compensation five years ago was a salary arrangement. If this had escalated at the cost of living rate over this period (e.g. 6 percent annually) the radiologist's average income would now be a little more than $65,000. In other words, each radiologist's current income is $35,000 higher than it would have been if they had been on a closed end arrangement. If this were only a two man department the $70,000 excess compensation could have been used to employ a third full-time radiologist to handle the increased volume of services.

If the hospital negotiator wanted to, he could also use income trends of all U.S. physicians rather than cost of living rates as his basis for comparison. *Medical Economics* magazine has regular surveys of private practitioners, called "Medical Economics Continuing Survey" which, for example, shows general surgeon's income increasing from $41,000 in 1968 to $68,000 in 1977, or roughly 7.8% per year.

3. Under the present contract with this hospital-based physician, have the operating costs of this department risen faster than operating costs of other major departments or total hospital operating expenses over the past three to five years?

4. Has the net operating margin of this department been gradually diminishing over the past several years because of increasing costs and/or operating inefficiencies? *Note:* Nationwide, according to the 1977 H.C.F.A. Study, the profit margins of the x-ray department, laboratory, EKG and emergency departments were respectively 28 percent, 21 percent, 50 percent and 7 percent.

5. Does the present contractual arrangement ensure the adequacy of professional staffing in relationship to volume of services? (This question relates to Objective 6).

Based on an historical evaluation of the ratio of the volume of services to full-time equivalent (F.T.E.) specialists providing these services, it might be possible to detect an undesirable trend that implies that the quality of professional services is being compromised. For example, if five years ago there were four F.T.E. radiologists performing 60,000 diagnostic procedures (*i.e.* 15,000 procedures/F.T.E. radiologist) and there are now five F.T.E. radiologists interpreting 100,000 procedures in this department (*i.e.* 20,000 procedures/F.T.E. radiologist), the hospital negotiator could easily argue that quality is now potentially less than it was five years ago with each radiologist trying to interpret 33 percent more x-rays than he used to. The chief radiologist would then have to concede that he was either overstaffed or less efficient five years ago.

3. Obtaining Commitment for Negotiations

After establishing and validating the hospital's negotiating position, the next step in the negotiation process is to ensure a full, unambiguous commitment to these objectives by the hospital's governing body and assign a hospital negotiator the responsibility and authority to manifest this commitment through the negotiations. As obvious as this step seems, it is surprising how often hospital negotiations fail for lack of such clear-cut commitments. More than a few hospital administrators have suddenly found themselves high and dry in the midst of difficult negotiations with their specialists when the board succumbed to a myriad of pressures and reneged on its original commitment to a position.

When this happens, not only are key objectives of the negotiations sacrified, but more often than not, the person negotiating on behalf of the hospital becomes a casualty because the credibility of his position and authority are irreversibly compromised in the process. It is not surprising, therefore, that many hospital administrators are reluctant to assume this role, especially if their boards show any signs of indecision or lack of willingness to be fully committed. It is also not surprising that several consultants recommend that such negotiations be carried out by the governing board rather than the hospital administrator.

The concept of commitment and its importance in effective negotiations is generally misunderstood by administrators and trustees alike. If properly used, it has extremely significant strategic value and if correctly delegated it can greatly enhance the hospital negotiator's bargaining position. It is my observation that even when a hospital administrator has developed a solid, justifiable position on contract negotiations, his success or failure frequently hinges on whether or not the trustees make a full commitment and not just understanding, acceptance or pledge of support for this position.

As paradoxical as it may seem, the first party to make (and openly manifest) an irrevocable commitment is often in a better bargaining position than the other party, even though this may severely restrict options for later compromise or a reduction in demands. For example, a board of trustee's commitment to renegotiate a physician's contract may become real and manifest when it sends that physician an official notice, without any conditions, that termination of the present contract will occur, say, 90 days hence, in accordance with the required notification period in the present contract.

Although the board is locking itself into this position by taking such action, the physician who receives this notice is not likely to regard it as a mere proposal or option by the board, but rather a clear, unconditional commitment to eliminate the present arrangement. If the board wanted to make its commitment even more conspicuously irreversible it could simultaneously notify its Medicare intermediary, rate review commission, and other affected third parties of this decision. The consequence of the board's making this first move is important; it restricts the range of subsequent negotiations significantly because the issue of whether the current contract remains intact is no longer negotiable and the hospital negotiator and hospital-based physician will focus their efforts on other issues that are negotiable.

Going one step further, the hospital governing body could also make a series of highly visible commitments to each of the nine objectives set forth earlier. For example, a public news release by the board indicating that it is committed fully to cost containment, including the elimination of open ended hospital-based physician contractual arrangements, would reduce the range of negotiations even further. The hospital-based physician may not be happy about this move by the board, but he knows, or should know, that he can't count on getting the board to release itself from such a highly visible commitment. Prior to this he may have been anticipating only a need to renegotiate his 25 percent of gross revenue arrangement down to say, 22 percent. Now, because of this move by the board to commit itself, even percentage of revenue arrangements are not negotiable because they are open ended.

Commitments, like threats, must not only be clearly perceived and understood by the other party, but they must also be credible to that party. In other words, the hospital-based physician must believe that the hospital and its board really have made an irreversible commitment, one from which they could not back down, even if they wanted to. In addition, unlike mere promises between two parties, commitments imply the existence of a third party to whom fulfillment is pledged. In one of the examples just cited, the board publicly announced its move through the news media, thereby putting its public credibility at stake if it failed to follow through. There is no question that this is very risky behavior but usually also a very effective prenegotiation strategy to restrict subsequent negotiations.

In this context we can now make a better decision as to who should serve as the hospital negotiator, and what degree of commitment this requires. Contrary to the suggestion of some consultants that this process be left at the board level, there may be better reasons to delegate the negotiation process to the hospital administrator. First, this is consistent with the newly emerging corporate structure in many hospitals, wherein the hospital administrator serves as the corporation's president and chief executive officer and, as such, is responsible for implementing all policy directives of the board.

Second, it allows the board to employ a wide range of bargaining tactics through its agent, the chief executive, that otherwise might not be available. For example, the chief executive can be given a very clear and inflexible set of objectives that don't allow room for concessions or latitude for interpretation; that is, the board can legitimately and conspicuously reduce the scope of authority of its executive, which is something it cannot really do to itself, at least with any credibility. Also it can employ "plateau bargaining" tactics whereby concessions may be gained from the specialist by the executive in its first round and then the board can insist on one or two more concessions in the last round — a ploy well-known by anyone who is quoted a low price by a car salesman, only to find out that the sales manager cannot accept quite so low an offer without a little more bargaining.

Third, and most important, if the hospital administrator makes the commitment to negotiate a certain position (or a series of objectives) effectively, the board of trustees in effect becomes the third party to whom fulfillment is pledged, and as a consequence the board itself may not need to manifest its commitment visibly to third parties outside the hospital — such as the public or insurance carriers or regulatory agencies.

If the hospital administrator is given full authority to negotiate, he could make it clear that his professional credibility (as an effective executive) with his own board is based on the fulfillment of his commitment in these negotiations. If it is clearly understood that the hospital-based physician cannot get the administrator released from this commitment to the board, and that the administrator also cannot get himself released, it has virtually the same strategic value as if the board itself made the commitment. For this to work, however, the board must be fully committed to its chief executive and cannot allow itself or any of its members to be vulnerable to pressures from the hospital-based physicians (or the medical staff or any other groups supporting the hospital-based physicians) to release the administrator from this commitment.

Unfortunately, even though this may be the ideal way to use the chief executive in the negotiation process, practical problems often arise. For example, one or more members of the board may have a personal friendship with the hospital-based physician or with another member of the medical staff who is supportive of the specialist's position. Or some trustees may have participated in previous negotiations with this specialist and now may be reluctant to admit the old contract should be revised dramatically. Some trustees may not be ready for a possible major confrontation with their specialists and may be quick to urge compromise — even if it leaves the chief executive in an untenable position.

Obviously, physician-trustees may be very susceptible to pressures from the hospital-based physicians. Any one of these factors, as well as several others, could give the hospital-based physician cause to suspect that the commitment is not absolute and irreversible so that in subsequent negotiations the administrator will have difficulty making his commitment to the position seem real and credible. In these circumstances his role may degenerate to that of a mediator (without binding authority) between the physician and the board, a situation that occurs frequently.

How, then, can a hospital administrator get his trustees committed to something to which they otherwise might reasonably be expected to acquiesce, especially when the heat really builds up? There are several strategies. First, the administrator must fully educate the board to all the inequities and inefficiencies of the current contractual arrangements. To the extent that projected real savings, such as $200,000 annually, can be quantified, the board's commitment can be heightened. In addition, he must convince the board that it has a corporate responsibility for ensuring these situations are resolved expeditiously and effectively. He must also make the board aware of the risks of an undesirable public exposure and third-party involvement if such contracts are not renegotiated.

To reduce the probability of the board's backing down if a serious confrontation should develop, the administrator would be wise to make a full disclosure of all possible negative outcomes and counter-strategies the hospital-based physician might resort to. For example, one negative outcome is the possible resignation of the specialist, and the administrator should not only prepare the board for this possibility, but he should know very clearly whether this is an unacceptable outcome as far as the board is concerned.

Another possible negative consequence is a confrontation with the medical staff, engineered by the hospital-based physician. The administrator should know exactly where the board will stand if this occurs, although he should also be able to convince his board that he has effective strategies and tactics to minimize or prevent such confrontations. It is incumbent on the administrator to convincingly demonstrate a negotiation plan, one that should achieve the desired objectives with minimal, unnecessary disruption to the operations of the hospital, but a plan which also totally depends upon the board's sustained commitment throughout the process.

Over and above these educational efforts, the administrator can employ other strategies to help the board stay committed. For instance, if the board is aware that past or present relationships will subject some of its trustees to personal pressures by the specialists or their advocates, the board might want to forego one or two of its official meetings so that during the negotiation process between the administrator and the physician no official change of position can be made by the board —an action that will probably deter the specialist from further pursuit of individual trustees. Again, as has been noted, even though it is risky, the administrator might urge the board to commit itself visibly to outside third parties so the hospital-based physician will be less inclined to try to persuade the board to back down on a position that is now linked to their credibility with this third party. If the hospital is part of a larger municipal, university or corporate structure or chain the administrator could encourage the local governing board to conspicuously manifest its commitment to a higher authority in the organization or the corporate headquarters.

Alternatively, the administrator could encourage a risk-sharing strategy whereby the board itself shares some of the risk of reneging on its own commitment to the administrator. For example, if one key, well respected member of the board is assigned to work with the administrator in some capacity relative to these negotiations, the board has an added incentive not to compromise the credibility of one of its own members by backing down from its original position. This is really a subtle strategy equivalent to taking hostages. Likewise, if the board agrees to delegate all decisions and commitments relative to the negotiation objectives and strategies to a restricted number of trustees (e.g. its executive committee) who have full authority to act, the risk of a hasty or unnecessary compromise by the full board will be substantially reduced; this also reduces the number of trustees who might be vulnerable to political or personal influences.

In addition to all the foregoing strategies which are aimed at making the board less subject to any incentives to concede on this issue, the administrator could seek ways to enhance his own value to the board and, thereby, increase the apparent cost of its potential capitulation. An extreme example would be a situation in which the administrator insists on an exorbitant severance pay allowance should the board renege on its original position before the negotiations are completed. The purpose of such a move is not to provide the administrator with greater security but rather to increase the cost to the board (even to the extent of being unreasonable) of not sticking to its commitment. An administrator who goes out on a limb (as such negotiations usually require him to do) and suddenly finds himself without support, not only loses this one issue but loses his credibility with the medical staff and even his own managers on future issues that may depend on the board's trust, confidence and support. A chief radiologist is not likely to be easily intimidated by contract negotiations with an administrator who just lost his board's backing on a pathology contract negotiation. It will be up to the individual administrator to determine how he can enhance his own position with his board prior to taking on such negotiations.

Under certain circumstances it may be appropriate for the administrator to delegate the negotiation role one step further — to his associate administrator or vice president. For example, when the chief executive officer/administrator also happens to be a physician he may be subjected to some extraordinary peer professional pressures not to negotiate aggressively and, even though he could overcome these, the negotiations might become significantly more difficult and prolonged than they would have been had a lay administrative officer been assigned the task.

In Catholic hospitals if the chief executive officer happens to be a Sister or a member of a religious order it might be more appropriate for the negotiations to be handled by a lay administrative subordinate of the chief executive for several reasons. The Sister/Chief Executive cannot effectively convey the impression that she is the appointed "executive" agent of the board in these negotiations who could not release herself from the board's commitment because as a Sister her real authority may even supersede that of the local board.

Once again, we have a situation where weakness and limited authority may actually be bargaining strength, even though we would normally expect the Sister/Chief Executive to have almost complete bargaining power by the very fact that she is in effect one of the hospital's real owners and, therefore, presumably there is no reason for her to delegate negotiations to anyone else. However, in situations involving "precarious partners", e.g. the hospital and its specialists or a company and its union, the owner may have the final authority but should avoid exercising it as it could become very costly to both parties to have to do so. There is less risk for both parties if negotiating authority is delegated away from the real owners.

Another reason the religious chief executive may wish to delegate negotiations to a lay administrative subordinate is that the latter clearly has a different incentive, as an employee-executive, to be aggressive and successful in the negotiations. A Sister/Administrator might not be expected by the other party to have this degree of commitment or this need to prove her executive credibility throughout the negotiations because she is not really an employee and also as a religious she may not be expected to exhibit aggressive negotiating behavior inconsistent with her past behavior or her Order's overall philosophy. This is not to say that a member of a religious order could not be a very aggressive and effective negotiator but rather that the other party's position will probably be developed on the assumption that this is not the case and could, therefore, result in more confrontative negotiations than might otherwise occur.

4. Assessing the Hospital Negotiator's Bargaining Power

If the administrator is assigned the responsibility of negotiating a new contract, he should evaluate his own bargaining position before he begins negotiations. One key element of an effective strategy is the enhancement of one's own bargaining power and a neutralizing or reduction of the bargaining power inherent in the opponent's position. Bargaining power is not equivalent to strength and authority; sometimes a person with limited authority has more bargaining power than a person with unlimited authority simply because the former has less latitude to compromise. Like any other form of power, bargaining power is most valuable in its potential; it can serve as a deterrent if the other party recognizes and accepts it. It should, therefore, be credible and visible (or made visible) to the other party or else it is meaningless. However, we should not forget that the other party has an incentive to neutralize our bargaining power and the more conspicuous our position, the more vulnerable it is to efforts to negate it.

Once we can identify our own potential bargaining power we can determine what strategies could be employed to enhance it. In addition, we must carefully assess our opponent's inherent bargaining power so we can decide how best to neutralize it. In some cases our bargaining power may be a function of his [the opponent's], usually in an inverse relationship. For example, the hospital administrator can usually consider his close relationship with his board of trustees as an inherent element of his bargaining power. However, if the hospital-based physician happens to be a member of the board or a close personal friend of the chairman of the board, the administrator would be foolish to think he has any bargaining power in this area. On the other hand, the administrator's bargaining power may be enhanced by virtue of the hospital-based physician's own weakness or vulnerability. For example, a specialist's poorly developed relationship with the medical staff may enhance the administrator's bargaining position because the specialist may not be able to rely on medical staff support for his position.

ADMINISTRATOR BARGAINING STRENGTHS

Here are some of the bargaining powers the administrator-negotiator may have, and what he can do to enhance them or at least make them more conspicuous and credible.

1. There is bargaining power inherent in his position as hospital administrator and chief executive officer.
2. Conspicuously good relationships between the administrator and his board, especially if it is a well-organized governing body with competent members and strong consistent leadership.
3. A clear commitment by the board in support of its administrator to negotiate close-end, reasonable contracts with its specialists.
4. A clear commitment by the board and its administrator to an aggressive cost containment campaign.
5. The respect and confidence given the administrator by the hospital's medical staff and its elected officials.
6. The respect and recognition given the administrator by community leaders, local village or municipal officials, and elected legislative representatives.
7. The respect of his professional peers and recognition achieved at a local, regional, state or national level on the basis of publications, committee appointments or other means; these help reinforce the administrator's professional credibility.
8. Good rapport with his counterparts in neighboring university hospitals or major teaching hospitals, either informally or through a formal medical school affiliation with the hospital; this improves the hospital's ability to recruit or attract qualified specialists.
9. A history of previous successful contract negotiations with hospital-based physicians, which clearly demonstrated the administrator's ability to negotiate aggressively and effectively.

10. Judicial decisions that reinforce the *Respondeat Superior* doctrine and virtually negate any claims of independent contractor status by most of these specialists.

11. Growing public and government concern over inequities inherent in such contracts and the likelihood of greater exposure and possible external regulation.

These represent only some of the commonest elements of his potential bargaining power. Specific circumstances will usually add to this list. For example, if the hospital-based physician has competent and ambitious professional subordinates, the administrator's bargaining position is improved because the specialist may be well aware of the fact that one of his subordinates could easily replace him if negotiations break down. Even if his professional subordinates are not well qualified, this, too, could enhance the administrator's bargaining position if handled properly.

For example, if the chief pathologist's two subordinates are foreign trained and lack board certification in either clinical or anatomical pathology, the administrator is in a strong position to challenge the quality of services performed in this area and can easily destroy the chief pathologist's potential argument that he needs to retain his lucrative percentage of revenue contract so he can keep (or continue to attract) highly qualified associate pathologists who otherwise would not accept employment under a salary arrangement with the hospital.

A good working relationship with the board can be made even more conspicuous if the board grants the administrator an apparent promotion just before the negotiations start. This might include a title change from "hospital administrator" to "president/chief executive officer." To enhance his bargaining power, the administrator might also deter the hospital-based physician from seeking support from the medical staff if he can take some action or actions that will augment the staff's respect and confidence in him or otherwise obtain its support. It is not difficult to find some minor issue that represents a nuisance or irritant to the staff that could be resolved by the administrator just prior to the negotiations; for example, a $2,000 expenditure for an expanded physician's parking lot may be all that it takes.

In some cases existing bargaining power could be used to make a strategic move even more credible. For example, if the board and its administrator have made a highly visible commitment to hospital cost containment, this not only serves notice on the specialists that their professional charges and income will come under scrutiny, but makes the following strategic threat believable.

The technic used by the administrator to get a pathologist to accept a salary and phase out of his current percentage-of-gross arrangement could be based on a cost containment effort to reduce all ancillary charges that have excessive profit margins built into them, such as the laboratory's and, if necessary, charges in other departments might have to be increased to cover their real costs. He might indicate that the hospital is contemplating a 25 percent cut in the profit margin of all laboratory procedures (or even a long-term freeze on increases in these charges), and naturally this will adversely affect the pathologist's current and future income as long as he is on a revenue sharing arrangement. On a salary he would obviously not be affected by this or any similar decisions in the future. This curious move, or the threat to implement it, will only be credible to the extent that the administrator's commitments to cost containment is perceived as sincere and resolute.

One critical element that is missing from the list of the hospital administrator's potential bargaining powers is a clear position by the American Hospital Association and other national and state hospital associations against open ended contracts with such specialists. Most hospital-based physicians have the benefit of strong professional society support for their preferred contractual arrangements, and this represents one potential bargaining position hospital administrators may have difficulty overcoming or even neutralizing with a counter-position by the hospital associations.

5. Assessing the Hospital-Based Physician's Position and Bargaining Power

In his prenegotiation planning the administrator should anticipate what position (and alternative positions) the hospital-based physician is likely to take in these negotiations, and develop his strategies and counter-strategies with this in mind. By this time the hospital administrator should know exactly what his own desired outcome is and by comparing his own position with the one he might expect the specialist to take he can determine how far apart the two starting positions may be. The wider the gap, the more resourceful he will have to be in devising a negotiating plan to achieve his objectives.

Based on some of the issues cited in Chapter II, the administrator can fairly accurately predict the method of compensation preferred by each specialty group, though in general there is now a very strong move toward direct billing, fee-for-service arrangements by almost all hospital-based physicians. But there may be differences in preferred alternatives if direct billing arrangements are not negotiable. For example, percentage of revenue arrangements are not likely to be primary or secondary preferences for emergency care physicians while this remains the preferred option with pathologists (with lease and direct billing close seconds).

Aside from compensation arrangements the hospital administrator should also be able to predict some of the preferences of various specialists relative to other terms of the contract, including administrative authorities, reporting relationships, determination of professional staffing requirements, private practice options, admitting privileges, and consultation privileges.

The special circumstances of each of 10 different hospital-based physicians, as were discussed in Chapter II, have important implications relative to their respective bargaining strengths and weaknesses. For example, we know that anesthesiologists are vulnerable to the extent that they have non-physician competition in the form of nurse anesthetists whom the hospital could employ as substitutes for anesthesiologists if they are not amenable to agreement. Even the J.C.A.H. standards do not require an anesthesiologist-director of this service; any physician can serve in this capacity. On the other hand, anesthesiologists have bargaining power inherent in their close working relationship (and probable support) with surgeons.

We also know that emergency care physicians may have a good bargaining position in support of their desire for direct billing arrangements on the basis that they do, in fact, have direct patient contracts, as well as vocal support from their professional association, A.C.E.P. On the other hand, the 1977 Mehlman *v.* Powell case negates some of their claims as independent contractors and also the fact that in most cases emergency care physicians need a hospital subsidy (a salary or a guaranteed minimum) because of the unpredictable volume of patients or marginal volumes in off-peak hours or days. The cardiologists' bargaining power is compromised by the availability of private on-line EKG interpretation services and neurologists could have their EEG interpretation role made obsolete by C.A.T. head scanning and certain nuclear medicine procedures.

The actual negotiation position a specialist takes, however, cannot be predicted solely on the basis of such issues. In part, his position might be influenced by his current contract, the *status quo* always being a strong bargaining position. His position may also be affected by what he perceives to be his own bargaining power, especially as it may relate to the hospital administrator's position and bargaining power. For example, if he has close contacts with several board members and serves on several board subcommittees (e.g. Planning, Joint Conference, etc.), he may feel he is in a very strong position and may feel confident enough to take a strong position for a direct billing, fee-for-service arrangement. If he is not so confident about his bargaining position he may try to renegotiate simply to keep his current arrangement even if it doesn't give him the same advantages as direct billing would.

At best, the hospital administrator can probably only make a good guess at the position the hospital-based physician might take in these negotiations. What he can do, however, is to assess the bargaining strengths inherent in this specialist's position and assume he will structure his negotiation posture around these.

PHYSICIAN BARGAINING STRENGTHS

The following represent some of the inherent bargaining strengths of most hospital-based physicians. These are only meaningful to the extent that the physicians demonstrate these strengths and make them credible.

1. Conspicuously good relationships between the hospital-based physician and the medical staff, especially if his department and its services are held in high respect by the staff. His bargaining power is greatly enhanced in this area if he is or has been an elected official of the medical staff or serves on key medical staff committees.
2. Close working relations with specific groups of physicians staff such as exist between anesthesiologists and surgeons, neonatologists and obstetricians and pediatricians, and cardiologists and cardiovascular surgeons.
3. A national or regional reputation and recognition in his specialty.
4. Membership in a strong and active professional society that has taken an unambiguous position on preferred contractual arrangements for its specialists.
5. Scarcity of well qualified, board certified physicians in this specialty, which might be compounded by an undesirable geographical location or the hospital's lack of prestige in the medical community.
6. His current contract and his tenure with the hospital which may enhance his bargaining position, at least to the extent that it helps reinforce his position to remain with the present arrangements and the *status quo.*
7. Precedent and prevalence of open-ended contracts at neighboring hospitals, and nationwide prevalence of percentage of revenue and direct billing arrangements.

8. Access to information regarding the profit margins generated by the emergency room, laboratory, x-ray department, EKG department, etc.

9. Participation in a private practice outside the hospital which ensures that he is not so dependent on the hospital as his sole source of income.His bargaining position is enhanced.

10. Finally, as has been noted, close professional or personal relationships with key members of the board or service on any major board committees. The extreme situation would be one in which the hospital-based physician is a member of his hospital's board of trustees, in which case it is very unlikely any contract negotiations would be occurring at all.

It should be added that just because one party may think he has bargaining power, this does not necessarily make it real. The other party has to recognize it as credible. For example, some hospital-based physicians may erroneously assume they have bargaining power in some situations: for example, the chief radiologist who believes such power flows from the fact that the employees in his department are loyal to him, or that he runs such an efficient department that he is virtually indispensable to the organization. Hospital-based physicians often make the mistake of assuming that they have bargaining power because their departments may be big income producers. It also is surprising how many hospital-based physicians actually believe that the revenue and profits generated by these departments are a consequence of their personal efforts.

6. Initiating Negotiations

Before discussing actual negotiating and bargaining strategies it might be appropriate to consider how such a sensitive issue as renegotiating contracts can be initiated. This might be a more serious problem than at first appears. On the premise that the *status quo* can be preserved by the party who can effectively ignore any initiatives for change, and assuming that most hospital-based physicians would prefer to keep their lucrative contracts intact, it becomes a real challenge to find a basis to open negotiations.

There are several ways the administrator and trustees might initiate the process of renegotiating their hospital-based contracts, but it should be remembered that this phase of the negotiation process creates an inherent double bind, or "Catch 22," for the administrator and trustees. The administrator cannot confront his hospital-based physician on the basis of excessive personal earnings, *per se,* because this would, in fact, be an admission that management has allowed such open-ended contracts that result in exorbitant compensations and that management should have put a stop to it long before it reached an inequitable level. On the other hand, the longer the administrator waits to initiate negotiations, the more difficult it will be to do so because the specialists may have an exponentially greater financial incentive to maintain the *status quo* with their current contracts. And once again the administrator incriminates himself if he tries to initiate a contract change on the basis of an even more exorbitant compensation level. The following suggestions represent some less self-incriminating ways the change might be initiated.

1. Because less than half of all hospital-based physicians in United States hospitals have no written contracts at all with their hospitals, this would be the easiest place to start. A good hospital attorney could articulate the need for a written contract to define these relationships, especially in the current

malpractice climate. Obviously, the administrator would be wise not to simply allow a codification of the existing informal or verbal agreement into a written contract, without making sure that he cannot use the opportunity to get the kind of contract he really wants.

2. Another obvious approach is based on the fact that many existing written contracts are old or otherwise obsolete, some even dating back prior to the enactment of the Medicare law. Any written hospital-based physician contract more than seven or eight years old might be found to be no longer viable in many respects, especially if the hospital attorney digs into it. The contract might be found to have questionable legal value in light of several judicial decisions that held hospitals liable for the actions of hospital-based specialists.

3. In some cases, changes in interpretations or policies by third-party reimbursement agencies might even be cause to revise contracts. In early 1975, for example, the Bureau of Health Insurance's interpretation of Section 2109 of the Provider Reimbursement Manual relative to emergency physician guarantees opened the door for hospitals to convert minimum guarantees to full-time salaried arrangements.

4. With some careful analysis it might be possible to find a contract that has inherently unreasonable, contradictory or inconsistent stipulations and clauses. For example, does the pathologist's contract (percentage of revenue, direct billing, etc.), allow him to share unfairly in the whole blood charges to patients, over and above processing that involves cross-matching, grouping and Rh typing? Or does his contract allow him to add unfairly on a charge for laboratory work sent to outside reference laboratories? Or does the radiologist's contract essentially allow him to participate in double billing on special procedures where both the radiologist and the neurologist, cardiologist or other specialist-attending physician are performing overlapping services for the patient, thereby, resulting in the radiologist and the specialist both receiving compensation for these services?

5. There is good cause to review and renegotiate many hospital-based contracts in light of rapid technological

changes that are adding a whole new range of hospital diagnostic services and, thereby, raising some questions as to which are the appropriate specialists to be using and interpreting these new diagnostic procedures. For example, in the last 10 years we have experienced a dramatic growth in diagnostic nuclear medicine. In some hospitals the pathologists have attempted to absorb these services under their control, on the basis that nuclear medicine involves "wet lab," radio immunoassay procedures; while in most cases the radiologists have retained nuclear medicine under their control, because this also involves "scanning" procedures.

Some hospitals have not allowed either radiologists or pathologists to take over the nuclear medicine department because in some respects nuclear medicine's diagnostic capabilities, if allowed to develop to their full extent, will, in fact, make obsolete many traditional x-ray services and some traditional laboratory services. To some extent the same applies to the introduction of other new diagnostic modalities, including ultrasound where, for example, it may become unclear whether the cardiologists or radiologists should interpret echo cardiograms. Again, the introduction of head and whole body computerized axial tomography may raise questions as to whether other specialists (e.g. neurologists and neurosurgeons) should be interpreting results rather than radiologists. Also to some extent C.A.T. procedures may make obsolete other routine x-ray technics and even some nuclear medicine procedures.

In any case, all these changes in technologies and new diagnostic methods may allow the administrator to step in to reevaluate the worth of the existing contracts and the distribution of responsibilities among various hospital-based physicians. In fact, the dynamics of this situation may be employed for strategic advantage by the administration in determining which specialists will have the privilege of using these new diagnostic modalities in the hospital.

6. Sometimes a change in the hospital's corporate bylaws or its medical staff bylaws may require a review of the hospital-based physician contracts for consistency. So, too, any ma-

jor changes in hospital or medical staff rules, regulations and policies may result in some aspects of the existing hospital-based physician contracts becoming obsolete, as, for example, when the medical staff adopts new policies relative to mandatory retrospective or concurrent medical audits in all departments and the current specialist contracts do not delineate this duty.

7. New demands from the Joint Commission on Accreditation of Hospitals, state hospital licensing and regulatory agencies, O.S.H.A., and other agencies may sometimes cause problems with the current contracts. State hospital licensing laws might, for example, require 24 hour in-hospital physician coverage in the emergency room or other requirements that the hospital might not be able to comply with under the present contract.

8. Another basis for re-opening contract negotiations is the cost containment initiative deriving from several quarters including legislators, the new consumer action groups, and rate review commissions. The board of trustees and especially its finance committee (and in some cases its cost containment committee, if it has one) would obviously have a legitimate concern for any inflationary and cost escalating components of the existing hospital-based physician contracts, and most such contracts obviously, are not cost effective.

As the board faces this cost containment issue *vis-a-vis* these hospital-based physician contracts, it does not have to focus directly on the high personal incomes these contracts have allowed; this is only a portion of the problem. Rather, the board should have the administrator look at all cost escalating aspects of these contracts, including their tendency to encourage overutilization of diagnostic services and serious departmental operating inefficiencies.

If the hospital does not employ a laboratory manager or x-ray department manager, the administrator can easily prove the value of establishing such positions for cost efficiency and improved operational management in the department and, as a corollary, thereby increase the hospital's direct influence and control over these areas. In addition, many hospital administrators might be surprised, after a careful cost accounting of some of these departments, that they do not produce the net revenue everyone supposed they did; and in some cases these departments have declining net revenues or even net losses because of the unfavorable terms of the contract with the hospital-based physicians.

This is especially easy to discover in hospitals that have sophisticated step-down indirect cost allocation methods and also where the hospital's Medicare (cost reimbursement) volume is relatively high. Under percentage of gross contracts that do not allow for a Medicare cost/charge adjustment, the hospital will likely be in a surprisingly poor net income situation in these departments. A cost conscious board with a good finance/cost containment committee can require an in-depth evaluation of all these issues and more likely than not give its administrator a legitimate opportunity to revise these specialist contracts.

9. Because hospital-based physicians frequently try to operate their departments as their own little fiefdoms within the hospital, it is usually not difficult to find some serious interdepartmental, administrative problems and these can serve as the basis for reviewing and revising contracts. For example, contrary to the hospital's established personnel policies, the chief pathologist and chief radiologist frequently give "their" technicians year-end bonuses, while such bonuses are not offered to other employees of the hospital. These department chiefs also tend to be more liberal in their interpretation and enforcement of hospital personnel policies in general, thereby, causing inconsistencies in those practices. So, too, purchasing procedures and policies of the hospital are frequently ignored and these may be a basis for administration's initiation of contract changes with those physicians.

10. An areawide survey of hospital-based physician contracts, undertaken by a regional or state hospital association, can also be a very valuable basis upon which the administrator can open contract negotiations. This type of survey, which also can be undertaken by a group of hospitals, if necessary, will typically reveal not only how their professional costs

compare with those of other hospitals, but also the physician staffing pattern at other hospitals in relation to their volume of services based on bed complements or other criteria.

Suffice it to say that there are several ways a resourceful administrator can legitimately initiate contract negotiations without being directly critical of the hospital-based physicians for the high levels of income they are earning or will be earning in ensuing years.

Whatever basis for opening the negotiation or renegotiation process is adopted, the current contract should be terminated with some specific deadline before negotiations start. This can best be accomplished through a formal, unilateral communication of this decision, preferably through registered or certified mail, which does not allow the other party to deny that he ever received the notification. The importance of a definitive deadline is that it puts a time pressure on both parties to renegotiate a new contract before the end of that period.

The deadline itself should not be negotiable. It should be reasonable and if a current written contract exists the deadline should be consistent with that contract's terms for termination. It should also be made absolutely clear that after the termination date the hospital and specialist have no legal relationship, formal or informal, unless in the meantime a new contract has been negotiated. Many hospital-based physicians are not aware that an implied legal relationship exists even in the absence of a formal, written contract and that the legal relationship ends only if the hospital so declares it. Therefore, in this sense it is not really critical whether the specialist currently has a written contract or not.

The legal relationship, implied or otherwise, can be terminated and a real legally important deadline can be attached to it. By this act, the hospital is committing itself and the specialist to this deadline, with the risk of no legal protection to either party after that date.

Finally, it is advisable that shortly after this contract termination letter is sent, a series of meetings between the hospital negotiator and the hospital-based physician should be scheduled so that a sequence of negotiations can be planned. For example, with a 90 day time limit it would not be unreasonable to set up a series of six meetings. We should recognize that within this 90 day period the specialist's bargaining power increases as time goes on because the hospital will have very little time to recruit replacements if negotiations totally break down in the last 30 days of his contract period.

With such a structured approach, the other party cannot legitimately argue, on the day before the present contract ceases to have any legal value, that he needs an extension or that he needs more time to consult with his attorney or accountant. Once the deadline commitment is extended, it proves that no real commitment really exists and the whole process might degenerate into bargaining over the need for further postponements. Incidentally, along these lines it might be wise not to initiate negotiations in the summer months because the hospital-based physician could legitimately force a delay on the basis that he has vacation commitments he can't break, or that his lawyer or his partner won't be available to consult with him on the negotiations.

One final warning and a very important one: After receiving notification that his present contract is to be terminated or at such time, thereafter, when the hospital-based physician finally realizes management is not likely to allow him to hold to the *status quo* (e.g. percentage of gross, percentage of net, lease, or other arrangements), he will very likely try to convert this situation to his advantage by developing a very strong position for direct billing. In other words, if he must change, he might as well go for the ideal solution. The wise hospital negotiator should anticipate a sudden mobilization of all possible resources by the hospital-based physician once he realizes the new contract negotiations are not just simple modifications to his current arrangement.

Incidentally, a clever anticipatory move by a hospital-based specialist would be to simply declare well in advance of any negotiations that should a new contract ever have to be negotiated he would view this as an opportunity to go on direct billing, implying that in fact he would benefit if the present arrangement was changed and, thereby, issuing a subtle threat to the administrator to leave it alone.

NEGOTIATING STRATEGIES AND TACTICS

1. Overview

By this point, the administrator-negotiator has basically completed the prenegotiation phase and is now faced with the actual one-on-one negotiating and bargaining. Based on several strategic moves that may have already occurred by this time, the range of the negotiations might be significantly reduced in scope to the advantage of the hospital negotiator. Several moves and commitments made by the board and the administrator may have resulted in a change or reduction in expectations of the hospital-based physician — even before the specific issues are put on the bargaining table. The physician who receives a letter of notice terminating his contract 90 days hence and then shortly thereafter receives a memorandum from the chief executive proposing a series of meetings with specific dates to renegotiate a new contract will know the board means business and will revise his expectations of his own position correspondingly.

From this point on, the administrator's strategy is nothing more than a plan of action to achieve the objectives he is committed to. By his selection of strategies, tactics and bargaining behavior, he can further alter the hospital-based physician's expectations of outcomes and, consequently, the choice of actions he takes (or doesn't take). The administrator's maneuvers are also aimed at further enhancing his own bargaining power and neutralizing the bargaining power inherent in the specialist's position.

What is curious about this process is that it all appears to be shadow boxing — much maneuvering for position but very few blows exchanged. Even communications are more often tacit and implied than direct and open. Each party has to work at finding out what the other's real expectations and intentions are. Consider for a moment the extreme difficulty both parties are faced with when the negotiations involve a specialist who has been caught with a $300,000 annual compensation level which is a consequence of an open ended contract that rapidly escalated out of control.

Although both parties may have a mutual interest in correcting the situation they cannot overtly collaborate in undoing it, because neither can find a graceful way to admit to his culpability in this situation. Unless the administrator is expressly prohibited by his board from allowing the present contract to be converted to a direct billing arrangement, this would be the only obvious solution that would benefit both parties, at least in the short run. If the board objectives do not include this option the administrator's strategy will probably have to include maneuvers to help the specialist resign.

In more typical negotiating situations, the strategies involve a series of subtle maneuvers that eventually get the two parties to a bargaining table with a restricted and manageable range of expectations. The remainder of this chapter will consider some of these strategic maneuvers.

2. Maneuvering Toward Conspicuous Outcomes

In almost every negotiating situation there are usually some obvious focal points for the outcome, whether we see them at first or not. For example, in discussing the hospital-based physician's bargaining power it was mentioned that the *status quo* of the present contractual arrangement is generally one obvious focal point of the negotiations, and as the negotiations get more and more complex the specialist may offer a tantalizing suggestion: "Look, why don't we just leave the contract the way it is — it's been working well all along . . . there's no need to change it." The temptation in the direction of *status quo* is so strong that it pays conspicuously to commit ourselves to change.

This notion of so-called "conspicuous outcomes" is discussed in detail by Thomas Schelling in *The Strategy of Conflict* and it is probably related to the fact that in bargaining behavior our own human nature tends to cause us to focus on obvious solutions and the more complex the issues, the more likely we are to try to simplify our efforts by looking for the most conspicuous outcomes. In the history of warfare it is remarkable how many more battles have been focused on hills or rivers and creeks than upon open plains or forests.

It is also surprising that after months of complex negotiations between management and a union, the final solution is often extremely simple and might have even been predicted before the negotiations started. So, too, when dollars or percentages or other quantifiable objects are involved in the negotiations we tend to gravitate to the obvious figure. For example, an administrator who proposes a salary of $77,000 should not be surprised when the final solution becomes $80,000. Another conspicuous outcome, which usually rises at the end of a hard session, is the old idea: "Well let's split the difference." Even precedent has powerful suggestive power as a likely outcome, so that the prevalence of an arrangement (e.g. percentage of gross) in a given area helps make it a conspicuous outcome. It is not the logic of these outcomes that causes us to gravitate toward them; it just seems so obvious or so simple a solution, especially when the whole situation becomes complex by contrast. In this context, the increasing prevalence and obvious simplicity of the direct billing option could easily make this a conspicuous outcome in contract negotiations.

From a strategic point of view it is important that the administrator recognize and use conspicuous outcomes to his own advantage, if he can, or develop tactics that prevent the other party from focusing on conspicuous outcomes that are undesirable. It may even be possible to create conspicuous outcomes by the way the problem is formulated or by the use of an agenda that focuses on certain key issues. If a barrage of data and information on the problems with the current contract is presented at the first negotiating meeting it might be possible to define the problem in such a way that the specialist will have virtually no choice but to hear the strong signals for a salary arrangement or other desired outcomes. The information may be made to speak for itself. Also, if the forthcoming negotiations can be made to be perceived by the other party as extremely complex, the hospital-based physicians may be more inclined to listen for the simplest solution, such as a salary.

If the administrator is unsuccessful in getting the problem defined so that it virtually suggests the obvious outcome close to his own preferred position he may have to throw up a defense to prevent the physician from trying to focus on the two obvious outcomes that are to his advantage — *status quo* and precedent. The administrator can usually bring forth a whole series of subsidiary issues to help drown out the conspicuous outcome signals from the other party.

In this very early stage of bargaining, the administrator's presentation of objective and quantifiable data can be useful in other ways. It gives the impression that the administrator is coming into the process loaded for bear, that he has done his homework, that he has information resources not available to the specialists, and to the extent that he can make his information sound credible the specialist cannot refute the data. For example, if the administrator simply presented the results of a confidential areawide survey of specialist's compensation the hospital-based physician could deny the validity of the data on the basis that the information was provided by fellow administrators.

This areawide information may be less subject to challenge if it was gathered by an independent management consulting firm. Otherwise, one ploy the administrator could use is to advise the specialist that he can pick any one (but only one) of the unidentified hospitals in the survey and the hospital's name will be revealed for the specialist to confirm the figure with his counterpart at that hospital. What usually happens, in fact, is that the specialist will not exercise this option, but if he does not he can no longer reject the validity of the data.

The administrator should make his initial presentation of data and issues so thorough that it covers not only all aspects of his own position but also the other party's expected position. This not only puts the other party on notice that the administrator knows all his opponent's potential arguments for his position, but it also deflects the specialist from later bringing up some of these now obvious points.

The more issues the administrator can bring into the negotiations, the better. If he floods the negotiations with a large number of issues it will give the impression that there is a vast difference between the two parties' positions, a common ploy used by unions when they come into the negotiations with an incredibly long list of demands. This maneuver has other values. It obviously discourages any hasty, simple offers like "let's split the difference"; there are now too many issues on the administrator's side to make this a beneficial move by the specialist. It also gives the administrator many more straw issues or secondary issues to later trade off for a major concession by the other party. The nine basic objectives of the hospital's position previously cited may provide enough issues and subsidiary issues to achieve this purpose.

3. Strategic Commitments and Threats — On Burning Bridges and Rocking Boats

Another area of useful strategies and tactics is that of commitments and threats, as has already been discussed in Chapter VI. In that prenegotiation phase, commitment served as a calculated maneuver to accomplish basically two things: The type and degree of commitment by the board of trustees was made manifest to reduce the range of negotiations before the bargaining process even started. In addition, the subsequent delegation of a restricted negotiating authority to the hospital administrator made his commitment to the board's objective more credible and, thereby, restricted the focus of negotiations even further; the hospital administrator's restricted authority manifestly makes him unable to make concessions in the bargaining process.

Both these examples of commitment are effective to the extent that they can modify the hospital-based physician's expectations and bargaining power relative to the negotiations.

The strategic value of commitments is indeed paradoxical. As Gerard Neirenberg points out in the *Art of Negotiating,* the principle of "burning bridges behind you" conspicuously heightens your own commitment and, thereby, deters or otherwise affects your opponent's expectations of what you will, in fact, do. It was a common military maneuver in the Middle Ages for a besieged army to burn the castle's moat bridge behind them as they ventured out to do battle with their attackers. This simple action made it very clear that they were committed to fight, and usually had the desired effect on their opponents. A union official who announces to his entire membership that he will win a $3 per hour salary increase in upcoming collective bargaining with management is basically doing the same thing.

In the area of negotiating with hospital-based physicians

several situations are ripe for the strategic use of commitments. A simple unambiguous commitment to an aggressive cost containment program by the board and its chief executive could serve notice on its hospital-based physicians that all contractual relationships will be subject to containment efforts. A commitment to reduce charges (or indefinitely freeze future rate increases) in all ancillary services may, if taken seriously, make all the hospital's revenue sharing specialists more receptive to salaried arrangements.

Also, as has been mentioned, the board of trustees can find ways to commit itself to the public or other third parties for the change of these contracts. It is worth noting that while the administrator can be made to have a commitment to a third party, *i.e.* the board, hospital-based physicians currently have fewer third parties they can commit themselves to. The hospital's medical staff used to serve this role but for all the reasons already mentioned the hospital-based physicians have less support in this area than ever before.

What the hospital negotiator will frequently discover during the negotiations with the chief anesthesiologist or radiologist or other chiefs is that his only commitment is apparently to his subordinate associates or partners — or perhaps only his wife. Although his reputation may be at stake only with such a small audience, it is significantly more difficult for him to demonstrate to his bargaining opponent [the administrator] what commitments he has made, or whether they are real or just expedient fabrications. It is also very difficult to truly pledge commitment to one's subordinates or even partners.

The strategic value of threats is very similar to that of commitments, and, so, too is their requirement for efficacy — the other party has to see and believe the threat. In this context threats are not to be considered a form of antagonistic or fighting behavior. Threats, like commitments, are made only with the intention of modifying the expectations of the other party, especially their expectations about our subsequent behavior if they chose not to heed the threat. A successful threat is one that is not fulfilled.

We don't have to look very far to find many examples of

threatening behavior that is beneficial. Mother Nature in her wisdom endowed the aggressive males of virtually all species with the good sense to back down from a fight when certain threatening behavior and cues are displayed. That most species have survived so long is testimony to the fact that threats are effective substitutes for real physical confrontation. It is also probably true that most negotiations break down and most wars start because of poorly manifested or poorly timed threats rather than the other way around.

The hospital-based physician negotiations will provide several opportunities for the effective use of threats while there are also ways to deter or neutralize threats from the specialist. One of the most obvious threats the specialist might make is a mass resignation of his associates and himself if they don't get their way in the negotiations. Presumably implicit in this behavior is a secondary threat that the medical staff would not put up with a loss of these specialists or even a temporary loss of their services. Even if the specialist does not threaten resignation he can threaten to seek the medical staff's endorsement for continued tenure under the present contract and, thereby, suggest possible confrontation between the medical staff and administration. The threat, whether implied or overt, basically says to the administrator: If you don't concede on this we will be compelled to take this action, and it is up to you, the administrator, to not make us have to take this action.

Long before such threats could be issued. a good hospital negotiator would have helped deter them by having communicated the board's intent and commitment to the medical staff's president, other elected officials and, if necessary, a few key, influential members of the staff and made this communication visible to the specialists. During the first stages of negotiations, the administrator could also have subtly implied to the specialists the ready availability of specialists from the nearby university or teaching hospitals who might be interested in a community hospital practice, or the H.C.F.A. data that revealed significantly lower specialist earnings on the East Coast and, by implication, the ease with which the hospital could recruit from that area if necessary.

A more interesting, but unquestionably risky deterrent maneuver by the administrator might be as follows. He might subtly imply to the specialist that up until now all aspects of the negotiations have been kept confidential, but should the medical staff be solicited for support, it is possible that critical personal income data might get out to the staff that would be harmful to both the specialists and the hospital. This appears to be a form of intimidation, but it is really a form of brinkmanship. Brinkmanship is an important negotiating tool, but is often misunderstood. What it is basically saying is: "Look, doctor, you and I are in this boat together and if you continue to seek outside support for your position, this boat we're in may start rocking and it may rock so much that it might be beyond my control to stop it from flipping over." Now the administrator didn't say "It *will* get beyond my control to prevent it from flipping." Rather he just said it "might" and he might not have any way of stopping it. If he were to use frankly intimidating behavior, he would have simply said "Look, doctor, I advise you not to make this a medical staff issue, but if you do, I'll be forced to produce all our data into the arena," which would have been riskier than he needed to make it. If the specialist is absolutely convinced that his earnings are not significantly higher than those of private-practicing physicians on the staff and if he is convinced that the staff doesn't think he is paying low salaries to his two or three associates, then he might run the risk of continuing to rock the boat. The administrator, however, didn't commit himself to anything by keeping this situation "iffy."

Some specialists may seek to deter the threat of a termination of their contracts (or any dramatic changes in them) by seeking support and sharing risk with a specific group within the medical staff, as, for example, anesthesiologists and the surgeons. Anesthesiologists are very vulnerable because they have non-medical competition in the form of nurse anesthetists and J.C.A.H. standards don't even require an anesthesiologist directing this service. However, their good working relationships with surgeons can serve as a real deterrent to threat, especially if most of the surgeons don't have surgical and admitting privileges at other hospitals. In this situation, anesthesiologists are in a strong position to threaten a walkout if they are compelled to accept undesirable contract terms, because surgeons will suffer economically along with the anesthesiologists if they ceased to provide their services.

Hospital-based physicians may also be able to deter threats of contract revisions if they can somehow convey to the administration that should the contract be terminated for any reason, they will, in fact, benefit because this will afford them an opportunity to go to a direct billing arrangement. If the administrator is not confident that he can prevent a direct billing effort by these specialists, he may be deterred from making any change in the current contract and the threat succeeds for the specialist.

In some situations the hospital negotiator can threaten to terminate negotiations with the chief unless certain conditions are agreed to. The threat becomes more credible if the hospital negotiator can negotiate with one of the chief's subordinates or associates. This is usually an extremely potent threat because the chief's apparent pledge of commitment to one of his associates would automatically be compromised or released if the ambitious associate showed any interest in usurping his boss in this role.

4. A Miscellany of Tactics

CONCESSIONS AND GAMBITS

Effective bargaining involves the proper use and timing of concessions. Every concession should be well thought out in advance and only offered when it has the greatest effect. Sometimes many small concessions can be offered in exchange for one big concession. In any case, whenever a concession is given, it should appear to be done reluctantly, and every concession made by the other party should be received unenthusiastically.

Gambits, by contrast, are apparently accidental concessions, that appear to be mistakes. They cause the other party to move where you want him to, based on his assumption that he will benefit by your mistake. It is possible, for example, that the hospital negotiator may make a $5,000 calculation error in the final proposed salary offer that might get the physician to focus on this apparent advantage he now has and, thereby, may cause him to think less of his other concerns about the arrangement.

PLATEAU BARGAINING

Plateau bargaining simply means giving a concession at a low level, and then when the final offer is made, the whole issue is submitted to a higher level where one or two more concessions may be obtained. For example, the hospital negotiator may succeed in getting the specialist to accept a salary arrangement based on a tentative offer of a certain dollar amount that might be approved by the board. The administrator must clearly indicate that he is authorized to negotiate a salary arrangement, but not fully authorized to commit himself on a particular salary. The administrator will then advise the physician that he needs board approval for, say, $120,000, while in the meantime the physician is accepting the principle of the arrangement. When he then advises the physician that the board can't accept $120,000, but will accept $110,000, the physician is more likely to accept it than not.

MEDIATORS AND AGENTS

When we think about negotiations with hospital-based physicians, we do not usually perceive a role for agents or mediators or other outside third parties in this process. Their use could, however, improve the whole process for both parties. Mediators are frequently helpful in suggesting an outcome that might be acceptable to both parties simply because the suggestion came from a third party and, thereby, helped get things off dead center. Also, they can play a very valuable role when two parties can't communicate openly or overtly coordinate their behavior, a common situation in negotiations between precarious partners. Neither the hospital administrator nor the specialist can openly discuss the exorbitant income the latter may be earning. Both are caught in a kind of double bind — if the administrator calls it exorbitant, the physician will be obliged to try to defend it or admit that he has been ripping off the system. If he can't defend it, then the administrator would have to admit that he sanctioned this income, or deny that it is really exorbitant. Bringing a mediator into the negotiating process may help both parties accept his suggested solution without having to expose the situation to explicit bargaining. Unfortunately, this is rarely done.

Mediators can also be helpful in making communications less than perfect, which may be useful under certain circumstances. I was involved in negotiations with a radiation therapist in Venezuela and even though he was a graduate of an American medical school a translator was employed. The translator, in fact, became a mediator of information and it allowed both parties to apparently be misunderstood long enough to find out what each other's real incentives were.

Lawyers as agents can be very valuable, especially on the side of the hospital negotiator. Lawyers unwittingly add more confusing details and legalese to every issue and, thereby, make the hospital-based physician more receptive to discussing the real issues. Lawyers also add a mysterious professional power to the administrator's position. It gives him added authority. On the other hand, the administrator should try to avoid the introduction of a lawyer by the other party, for basically the same reasons. The negotiations may deteriorate into a discussion of specific details and phraseology of the contract rather than keeping the real issues in proper focus.

DIVIDING TO CONQUER

In some circumstances, it may be wise to attempt to bring all the associates into the negotiations and, thereby, expose the chief's apparent commitment to them. This will usually be resisted by the chief for obvious reasons and it can also be risky to have to face five specialists rather than one.

STRAW ISSUES

As noted earlier, straw issues are important. The administrator should be prepared to make some minor issue seem of great importance so when he goes to offer this issue as a concession, it appears to the other party to be a major concession. An administrator may also create straw issues that don't even exist.

BLUFFING

This is a very risky tactic that is probably not worth the effort. One exposure of a bluff may compromise the credibility of the administrator so badly that future real threats may be ignored by the physician.

UNCERTAINTY OF EXTERNAL INFLUENCES

One major tactic available to the administrator is the basic uncertainty about governmental regulation in this industry. Many legislative changes appear imminent and the administrator can frequently refer to the intent of upcoming bills that might support his case — even if the bills are subsequently defeated. The Rostenkowski cost containment bill was defeated, but it still has some use for the negotiator, because it can be cited as an indication of the way legislators appear to be heading. The same can be said of the defeated 1978 Medicare revision bills, including the section of that bill that would have disallowed Medicare reimbursement to all hospital-based physicians operating on revenue sharing arrangements.

JUDICIAL TRENDS

Another useful tactic is the potential negotiating value of certain judicial decisions that favor the hospital's position, especially in the area of the "independent contractor" concept. In addition, just having a good, solid grasp of such decisions is usually intimidating to the other party, especially since many physicians do not have a good grasp of legal issues to begin with.

5. 32 Classical Obstructions and Counter-Arguments

The following list represents some of the common objections the hospital-based physician employs during the negotiations, and the administrator-negotiator would be well advised to be prepared for them. This list was derived from actual experiences in negotiating contracts with pathologists, radiologists, emergency physicans, nuclear physicians, cardiologists, respiratory/pulmonary physicians, hospital-based physiatrists, and others. Now that the A.M.A. sponsors a program on negotiating technics, it is possible that many more obstructions and tactics will be used in the negotiations.

Each of the following statements is typical of those made by the hospital-based physician to the administrator-negotiator during the early phases of the negotiations. Some of these, obviously, are really maneuvers to stay with the *status quo;* some are predicated on quality issues that may be difficult for the administrator to respond to; some are subtle threats.

1. "I simply can't accept a salary contract because I won't be able to attract high quality pathologists who are willing to work for hospital salaries. . . and you certainly don't want anything less than high quality pathologists for our hospital."

Comment: This statement raises a quality issue, implying that the pathologist would be forced to compromise quality under a salary arrangement. However, the pathologists is not saying that he, himself, is opposed to salaries, but that other pathologists are and in a sense he has to live with market conditions.

This could be a fairly effective move because he is forcing the decision to potentially compromise quality back on the administrator; also the pathologist avoids having to take a position against salaries on his own behalf. The best countermove might be for the administrator to assure the pathologist that he would be authorized to pay a salary to his associates, if qualified, up to his own salary level (after it is agreed upon) and presumably the hospital could attract or retain associate pathologists as good as he is. Such a response takes advantage of the implication in the pathologist's statement that he is not opposed to salaries and that, therefore, there should be other very competent pathologists on the market who are also not opposed to salaries.

2. "Salary arrangement for me and my staff pathologists are not acceptable because fixed salaries don't offer any incentive whatsoever."

Comment: This statement might be more effective if made by a radiologist, but pathologists are very vulnerable on this point. The hospital negotiator should cite the testimony given at the 1970 Senate Anti-Trust and Monopoly Committee hearings, *i.e.* 85 to 90 percent of the laboratory's output is not related to the pathologist's efforts and, therefore, no incentive may be required for this output. Also, the administrator should point out that the hospital's salary arrangement would provide for annual reviews for cost of living and merit adjustments, thereby, giving pathologists an incentive with regard to the greater part of their supervisory and quality control duties.

3. "I'm incorporated, so I can't accept a salary from the hospital." Another variation of this is: "If I were to accept a salary, I'd lose my ability to participate in income-deferring programs that save me a great deal in taxes." A second variation: "I'm incorporated and if I accept a salary, I'll lose many of the tax benefits and write-offs I presently have."

Comment: This defense is based on a lack of understanding of what it means to be incorporated as well as an effort to equate fixed compensation with employment by the hospital. Obviously, someone can't be employed by two corporations simultaneously. The proper response to this would be to indicate first that there are several advantages to being employed by the hospital that could well exceed private corporate status. For example, annuity programs that the hospital can offer (as a not-for-profit, charitable enterprise) may exceed the income deferring potential of the Kehoe plan and other options available to for-profit corporations. In addition, the administrator could offer a "concession" and allow fixed contractual payments to the specialist or his corporation in lieu of a salary *per se,* and indicate that this would not be much different from the way the hospital purchases other expert services.

4. "I don't want some outside governmental rate review commission telling me what professional charges I can make and that's what will happen if I don't go to direct billing soon." *Variation:* "As long as my charges are in any way tied to the hospital, my professional fees could get regulated like hospital charges — that's why I need to bill patients directly."

Comment: This is the position most professional societies are now trying to educate their membership to understand, and it is a strong argument indeed.

The hospital negotiator's response could include the fact that in a test case in Maryland the state's rate review commission was explicitly denied the right to regulate hospital-based physician's fees. However, this is risky because that decision also implied that hospital-based service charges are not really hospital costs, and further it is very probable that rate review commissions will obtain this authority eventually.

A second response would include the fact that insurance companies (and maybe even Medicare) may not in the future accept direct billing arrangements. Cite the Pennsylvania Insurance Commission's strong stance against direct billing. Also, given the fact that direct billing typically adds another $2 to $3 cost per billing (for a collection agency) this could significantly increase the cost of services and invite mandatory cost containment legislation. For example, 80,000 x-ray procedures could add an additional $160,000 or more to these costs.

5. "Are you opposed to direct billing because you don't trust me to charge fair and reasonable rates for my professional services?"

Comment: This is usually a fairly effective maneuver, *i.e.* to raise the question of trust and force a yes or no answer. It creates a double bind for the administrator. If he answers "yes," it compromises further negotiations because it implies the hospital-based physician cannot be trusted. If he answers "no" then he will have to come up with other reasons why the hospital insists on combined billing.

He could argue that direct billing will mean additional collection costs for such services, while the hospital's present collection services are more cost efficient. But more importantly, he could argue that it is really not a question of whether he trusts the physician; it's what the public and other third parties think, and there has been enough negative publicity over hospital-based specialists' exorbitant earnings to warrant some distrust by these outside parties.

Cite the H.C.F.A. Study and the 1978 Senate hearings which exposed personal incomes of $500,000 under direct billing arrangements and situations where direct billing resulted in five-fold increases in earnings over former arrangements. The administrator's position should be that he no longer has the right or authority to delegate fee regulations to the specialist himself, as long as the public expects the hospital to maintain this control.

6. "Combined billing is O.K., but we want to determine our own charges because those are professional charges and we're the ones who know how much professional skill and time is required for each type of procecure."

Comment: This is a slightly different tactic from those mentioned earlier. He is now saying only physicians know what professional skills are involved and, therefore, only they can determine what is an appropriate charge. The best move the administrator could take would be to capitalize on this by maneuvering for the implementation of a relative value structure developed or revised by the specialists. This would take the mystery out of the charges and would allow the administrator to eventually control the overall dollar unit value instead of getting into the area of determining what each procedure is worth professionally. The hospital-based physicians will undoubtedly resist this move for relative value scales for this very reason — it totally defuses this argument.

7. "I don't think you have the right to determine or even approve my professional charges any more than you have for

an internist or surgeon in private practice."

Comment: This is a simple effort to make an analogy of hospital-based physicians to physicians in private practice. It is easy to overcome by citing the differences between the hospital-based physicians and private practitioners, *i.e.* the hospital provides the former with equipment, staff, a guaranteed supply of patients, and a restricted closed staff franchise; also the hospital assumes legal liability for all the services provided in these departments.

8. "Separate billing will help your cost containment efforts because under this type of arrangement you will reduce your professional expenses on your books by $600,000 each year, and you'll look a lot better on your balance sheets."

Comment: This is an attempt to take advantage of the administrator's commitment to cost containment. It assumes, though, that the administrator only cares about reducing hospital costs or apparent costs, simply by transferring these professional fee costs off the hospital's ledger. The administrator should react by indicating that this is irresponsible — transferring costs is not containing costs. Furthermore, he can negate this cost containment argument by citing the additional collection costs to the public and the fact that such arrangements can cause as much as a 500 percent escalation of professional charges.

9. "This separate billing contract is O.K. because it allows fee-for-service, but even better for you is to let us bill directly. That way the hospital doesn't even have to get involved in any of the billing and you won't have to hire any more collection employees in your business office; besides, you won't have to worry about any bad debts from professional fees. This will save the hospital a lot of money."

Comment: Again, the appeal is to cost containment, but again, it can be easily negated. The administrator should explain the inherent efficiencies of the hospital assuming the billing functions as a simple extension of its current role and that no employees would have to be added to carry out this function.

10. Emergency Room Physician: "I have direct patient con-

tacts and render care directly to patients — so I should have the right to bill patients directly, like any other physician who has a physician-patient relationship." (Anesthesiologists also frequently take this position.)

Comment: This is basically the A.C.E.P. position and represents an effort to distinguish this specialty from other hospital-based physicians who do not have such direct contact, such as pathologists and radiologists. The administrator's response should relate to the hospital's role as seen by the public it serves and the importance of the emergency department as a hospital service to the public. It should stress that with the public obligation goes the obligation to regulate professional fees.

The Mehlman *v.* Powell case could be cited to demonstrate that the hospital is being held liable for the services of emergency physicians on the basis that the public perceives the emergency physician as being employed by the hospital. Also, he could neutralize the apparent distinction between emergency physicians and pathologists or radiologists by pointing out that patients do not have a free choice of emergency physicians nor can the emergency physicians provide their services without hospital-provided support staff, equipment and space.

11. "You can't require us to use a relative value index for setting our charges, because this is illegal, price fixing and the ACR (and CAP) got a ruling on this."

Comment: Hospital-based physicians do not usually favor the use of relative value scales because this takes the mystery out of professional fee determination and makes aggregate fees subject to indirect control by means of the dollar value assigned to the unit. Many specialists were, therefore, delighted by the 1977 Justice Department's consent decree. However, the decree did not prohibit hospitals from using these scales. It just prohibited professional societies from promulgating them — a decision overruled in 1979.

12. "Using a relative value index in establishing our professional charges is not acceptable to us; we want these professional charges to be based on areawide customary charges by

other radiologists (pathologists, emergency physicians, anesthesiologists, etc)."

Comment: Hospital-based physicians prefer to use customary areawide charges as the basis for their professional fees because this essentially puts fee determination outside the control of the hospital. It also allows them to participate in inflationary escalation of such fees because keeping up with areawide charges is a vicious cycle. Also, since some hospitals continue to allow open ended contracts, the use of customary fees permits the specialists to benefit from the irresponsible fee escalations that may occur when, for example, neighboring hospital radiologists on percentage of gross contracts automatically share in their hospital's x-ray department rate increases — usually at a double digit inflation rate.

This is why it is so strategically important for a hospital administrator who is breaking areawide precedents (by eliminating percentage of revenue contracts and establishing a combined billing arrangement) not to let the potential advantage be lost by permitting charges to be based on areawide rates; it could end up being only a Pyrrhic victory for him.

13. "I believe our state's professional statutes prohibit me, as a doctor, from receiving a salary from the hospital."

Comment: This is the old "corporate practice of medicine" position. Although conditions may vary in each state, there is usually no basis for this argument, especially as it applies to charitable organizations. The specialist may be paying salaries to his junior associates and this could be quickly thrown back at him. Also, a fixed compensation arrangement could be substitued for the term "salary," and, thereby, negate this defense. Every administrator would be well advised to know his state's statutes in advance so he can take a strong position.

14. "I think it's against the law for a corporation to profit from a doctor's services and that's why I'm opposed to accepting a salary here".

Comment: This is basically the same position as No. 13 except the implication here is that the hospital is profiting from the specialist. Make it quite clear that just the opposite is the case. For example, there is no question that the specialist is profiting from the work efforts of the nursing or technical support staff in these departments. Even secretarial staff and automated equipment (e.g. automated x-ray film display units, automated word processing units, etc.) save the specialist professional time and allow him to be more efficient and, thereby, increase his output, which, in turn, increases his personal compensation.

15. "If you're so concerned about our making too much money, I'd suggest we leave our pathology contract on a percentage of gross basis but maybe we can agree upon some upper limit each year."

Comment: This is basically a *status quo* move with a minor concession — an upper limit. Theoretically, an upper limit would meet the administrator's desire to put an end to an open-ended arrangement, but it simply is not logical. On what basis, for example, could a pathologist (or radiologist) reason that the first procedure performed in the year is professionally worth 25 percent of the charge, while the same procedure performed at the end of the year would be done with no professional charge at all if the upper limit had already been reached.

This concession is important and should be used for all it is worth. For example, it would be very interesting to see what upper limit he might suggest, and if this is reasonable, the administrator might be able to convert this concession into a simple fixed compensation arrangement (equivalent to a salary), if it can't be converted directly to a salary. This concession might be accepted as the first step toward a salary arrangement, especially if the offer were to come from radiologists (rather than pathologists for whom there is no justifiable basis for any kind of revenue sharing arrangement).

16. "I agree that under our present percentage of gross arrangement we (the radiologists or pathologists) benefit a little every time you, the hospital, increase charges in our department (to cover the increasing costs of supply, equipment and wages) but don't you think that we are entitled to increasing professional compensation, too. . .our cost of living goes up every year, too, just like the employees in this department."

Comment: The administrator should have solid facts in

hand to demonstrate that they have benefited significantly more than just "a little." It would be fairly easy to show how much "windfall" profit the specialist has made over normal cost of living increases in the past five years.

17. "It's not fair to say we *[pathologists]* can't continue with percentage of gross, when you're allowing other hospital-based physicians, radiologists, to receive a percentage of gross." *Variation:*. . .when you're allowing hospital-based anesthesiologists to bill their patients directly."

Comment: This is a strong bargaining position for the specialist. Internal precedent is hard to refute and will force the administrator into having to show how this department is different from others that are allowed to continue on revenue-sharing arrangements. Alternatively, he can point out that contract renegotiations will be occurring with all specialists who have open ended contracts, but he had better not say this if other specialists have not already been put on notice.

18. "It's not true the pathologists are only directly involved in 10 percent of the output of the laboratory (*i.e.* surgical pathologic procedures and autopsies); we're responsible for the quality of every test performed in the laboratory and we'll be sued if we don't produce correct results. Therefore, there is no reason we shouldn't get a percentage of gross or other form of professional compensation for each procedure performed in the laboratory. We're legally responsible for everything."

Comment: In addition to the reasons cited in Chapter I why this position is not valid, the administrator can defuse the implied legal argument in this by simply asking the pathologist if he and his associates provide malpractice/liability coverage for all the technicians in the department as well as the hospital itself. Also the pathologist could be asked to cite just one judicial decision that ever held a hospital pathologist responsible for the negligence of the technical staff. The administrator can cite many such decisions to confirm that the hospital, not the specialist, is legally responsible for all professional and paraprofessional services rendered in the laboratory, the x-ray department, the emergency department and others.

19. "Look, our department (x-ray or laboratory) is one of

the biggest revenue producers you've got in this hospital; and if your proposed contract changes are not satisfactory, you might compromise this high income source."

Comment: Hospital-based physicians believe their bargaining position is strong because they are income producing departments. What they fail to understand is that this would be true no matter who the chief of the department was. This simple fact is a surprisingly common blind spot for these specialists, and the administrator can easily make this clear.

20. "Our professional costs might be higher than those of neighboring hospitals, but that's because the quality of our work is higher; and we also provide better coverage (hours and days of service) than other hospitals."

Comment: The administrator cannot argue with the quality issue, *per se*. He should, however, be prepared in advance to be able to challenge the issue of better coverage, which he can do through a survey of areawide hospitals.

21. "Maybe my compensation this last year was a little higher than pathologists (radiologists) in this area, but don't forget that I personally contributed $5,000 to your hospital building program this last year and that was out of my own so-called high personal income." A *variation:* "Well, out of my own pocket I gave some of our best technicians bonuses this last year and I personally paid for a departmental picnic and a Christmas party." *Another variation:* "I personallly purchased $30,000 worth of equipment for my department over the past couple of years and I think this should have been taken account of when you compare my compensation with other pathologists (radiologists)."

Comment: Again this tactic is aimed at making the compensation data invalid because it does not reflect these donations. This is also a maneuver to remind the administrator how loyal to the hospital the specialist has been. It also explains why an administrator should never allow a specialist to make contributions for equipment for his own department: he'll use it as a bargaining issue when his excessive compensation level becomes an issue. The wise administrator will always insist that a contribution from specialists be made to a general hospital fund, or, at most, to a department, but never for specific equipment. If a pathologist is allowed to purchase a Coulter S out of his own income, this confirms his own belief that the laboratory is his department and not a hospital department. Also, if he is allowed to give his technicians special bonuses inconsistent with personnel practices of the hospital, he is manifesting his assumption that the laboratory is his department. The administrator should point out that this is totally inappropriate management behavior on his part and inconsistent with the organization's policies. An administrator who allowed his specialist to purchase major equipment for his department or who sanctioned out-of-pocket bonuses to employees has very poor bargaining power in this area.

22. "The hospital's making more than 30 percent profit in my department, and you're trying to make an even greater profit by this proposed contract." *Variation:* "Don't tell me you can't afford to continue to provide my current level of compensation — you're making 30 percent profit off my department." *Variation:* "How can you talk about containing costs here if you're charging 30 to 40 percent more for these services than it costs? Are you going to cut out that fat, too?"

Comment: This could be one of the Achilles' heels of the administrator's position. Such profit margins are no longer justified. With the vast majority of patients covered by third parties there is very little reason for costs and charges not to be close in all areas of the hospital. The best an administrator can do in this situation is to try to make a convincing argument how these professional contract savings will be used to reduce charges throughout the hospital, including this particular department.

23. "The medical staff has been satisfied with the quality of services my associates and I have been providing and I'm sure you wouldn't want this to be compromised by any changes in the present contract that has allowed us to provide high quality services."

Comment: The is one of the commonest and most effective maneuvers to maintain the *status quo.* It will be hard for the administrator to get a clear answer from the specialist as to how a new contract will compromise quality of services. This assumption may even be believable to the medical staff and it might be difficult for an administrator to prove that a change could not possibly compromise the quality of services. To anticipate and prevent this subtle threat, the administrator should make sure the specialist is aware in advance that the president of the medical staff and other key officials are fully aware of the board's commitment to change and the administrator apparently already has the staff's understanding and acceptance of the need for this change.

24. "This proposed contract is unacceptable and will not be approved by the medical staff."

Comment: This is the overt threat to seek support from the medical staff to prevent a change. It is a bad move by the specialist, especially if the board has openly manifested its commitment to change the contract because not only is the likelihood of full support from the medical staff very questionable these days but it is possible that the medical staff might find out about these specialist's own personal earnings.

25. "Since the board of trustees approved this contract many years ago and has obviously continued to approve of it since then, why not just leave it as it is?"

Comment: This is another plea for the *status quo* but it attempts to remind the administrator that the board sanctioned the current contract and the administrator could just leave it as it is. At this point, the administrator should advise the physician that he really does not have the authority to make such a concession and furthermore, the board is committed to change because the board initiated these renegotiations.

26. "This proposed contract is unacceptable and I'll only negotiate a new contract directly with the board of trustees."

Comment: The physician is failing to perceive that the board has made a commitment and has delegated this to the administrator. The administrator's possible response: "Doctor, I'm sorry but the board as a whole acted on this issue of renegotiating a contract, and they are not scheduled to meet as a full board till after the termination date of your present contract. Nor do I have the authority to extend your current contract beyond that date. In the meantime I would suggest we continue to work on the revision to see if we can find an acceptable arrangement before your contract expires. If we can, fine — your time and my time will be worth the effort. If we don't, I'll make arrangements for professional coverage from the University Hospital for that interim period."

27. "I'm incorporated, so I'll have to bring my corporate counsel into these negotiations." *Variation:* "I will not meet to negotiate my contract unless my attorney is present." *Variation:* "My attorney (and tax consultant) are out of town for most of the summer, and I need their advice before I can meet with you."

Comment: The threat to use legal agents in the negotiation process is usually very effective. All the administrator can really do is refuse to have such a meeting, or insist on the hospital's legal counsel also being present. The counter-threat of bringing in the hospital's attorney is not usually of any consequence; it doesn't often deter the physician from involving his lawyer. The administrator could suggest the two attorneys meet to discuss their relevant concerns while the administrator and physician continue to meet to negotiate over other issues.

28. "I'm in a partnership, so I don't have the full authority to accept the terms of the contract you are proposing . . . you'll have to meet with my partners as well."

Comment: This is generally a very naive move by the specialist because it leaves him wide open to a strong countermove by the administrator, and a possible loss of his role completely. The administrator's response could be any of the following. He could indicate that he thought he was negotiating with this specialist because he believed he had the authority to represent his partners and that he was also under the impression, until now, that the hospital had delegated the authority to direct these services to this specialist — not five men. The administrator could then suggest he would be glad to meet with any of the other associates who might better represent them all, or alternatively he would be willing to consider meeting with each separately to work out individual contracts of service with the hospital.

What the doctor did by making this statement was to imply the use of his partners as a "third party" to whom he is committed and if he makes this kind of statement after the first few negotiation meetings (rather than announcing it at the beginning of the first meeting) it seems to suggest that the administrator has him trapped; and now rather than go back and face his partners with a bad option, he'd prefer to release himself from the commitment by extracting himself as their delegated negotiator.

29. "I'm sorry, but I don't think the terms of this proposed contract are consistent with or acceptable to the position of my professional society (e.g. College of American Pathologists, American College of Emergency Physicians, American College of Radiology, etc.)."

Comment: The administrator can cite the various antitrust rulings that prohibit the professional societies from taking any kind of discriminating action against members who chose to operate under arrangements not recommended by the society. Therefore, the specialist will be obliged to argue why he supports his society's position.

30. "Even the American Hospital Association supports my type of contract and doesn't recommend one type of contract over another."

Comment: The A.H.A. does not favor lease arrangements and does favor professional fee regulation by the hospital relative to separate billing arrangements. Beyond this, there is no further defense the administrator can raise.

31. "I don't consider your data from other hospitals objective or correct and I don't accept this as a basis for these negotiations."

Comment: This is an effort to make the data appear invalid and, thereby, reduce the administrator's bargaining power. The most obvious way to prevent this challenge is to have the survey carried out by a management consulting firm.

32. "You don't have the authority to prohibit me from setting up my own private x-ray service (or laboratory) within five miles of the hospital. This is a monopolistic practice on the hospital's part."

Comment: This is not a very critical issue with pathologists; they usually cannot become competitive with the hospital anyway because large private reference laboratories are very competitive. For radiologists, it is critical because they could have a significant impact on the hospital, and once they have the right to establish a private practice, their bargaining power in all future negotiations is significantly enhanced. There is no restraint of trade involved here and the administrator should seek the hospital attorney's legal opinion on this matter before the negotiations. This is essentially like any other conflict of interest situation.

6. Detailed Case Example

Renegotiating a Percentage of Revenue Contract to Salary

This case and the following one are not related. But the same basic principles apply to both situations. For ease of description some common factors have been introduced. Each case will be presented in the following format:

A. Initial situation
B. Position — Objectives to be taken in the negotiations.
C. Strategy — Negotiator's original plan of action to achieve these objectives.
D. Outcome — What the end product was.
E. Actual Negotiations — What, in fact, occurred between C and D.

The initial situation is basically the same for both cases. The objectives varied somewhat, and because the same hospital negotiator was involved in both situations, basically the same strategies were developed for both negotiations. The outcomes varied dramatically and the actual negotiating process also varied significantly.

A. Initial Situation

In the early 1970's, a newly appointed administrator at a 420 bed community hospital in the West evaluated current professional earnings of his radiologists and pathologists; both groups were operating under percentage of gross revenue contracts. He discovered that $344,000 was being earned by three pathologists.

The administrator undertook a confidential areawide survey of the eight nearest hospitals to determine if such contracts and levels of earnings were prevalent in the area. He discovered some initial resistance from neighboring administrators to providing their data. They appeared reluctant to provide information that might reveal how they had allowed their own situation to get out of control, and did not want any information to get out to the public. Only the chief executives were involved in providing the information and they were assured that specific hospitals would not be listed in the survey results.

The study confirmed that both pathology and radiology contracts were yielding relatively higher earnings than those of most other hospitals even though percentage of gross was the commonest arrangement. The pathologists' compensation was significantly higher, ranking second highest out of nine area hospitals.

An internal survey confirmed that the pathology department was experiencing a gradual decline in profit margin — a result of increasing operational costs with no relief in the professional expenses. The department also had excessively high utilization rates (*i.e.* diagnostic procedures per day) compared with those of other similar hospitals in a Blue Cross regional sampling.

The administrator presented the data to the chairman of the board of trustees, who in turn called an executive committee to discuss the findings. The administrator recommended that both contracts be terminated and renegotiated.

B. Position — Objectives

In dealing with the pathology situation, the board's final position was to negotiate for straight salaries or fixed compensation arrangements and eliminate the percentage of revenue contract. No specific objectives were established beyond this and it was left to the administrator to consider what other issues needed to be resolved, including the maximum salary levels that could be offered.

C. Strategy

To achieve this objective, the administrator developed the following plan of action or strategy:

1. After consulting with the hospital's attorney about the terms of the current contract, write to the pathologist, notify

him of a termination of the present contract before any discussions are held with the chief pathologist and arrange a series of meetings over the subsequent 90 day period to renegotiate a new contract.

Reasoning: This will make the decision appear irreversible.

2. Notify the president of the medical staff that the contract with the pathologists would be renegotiated, based on a commitment of the board, but that this would not affect the quality or range of services presently provided by this department; nor would it be necessary to bring this before the medical executive committee because it only relates to method of remuneration.

3. Make sure the chairman of the board agrees to meet with two trustees who might be approached by the chief pathologist to obtain their commitment to make themselves unavailable for any personal meetings or discussions with the chief pathologist about this issue. One trustee is a close neighbor of the chief pathologist and the other serves as chairman of the medical relations committee and was involved in negotiations with this pathologist eight years ago.

4. At the first meeting with the chief pathologist (to be set up within two days after he receives notification of the termination of his contract) the following position will be taken:

4.1 We, the hospital, looked at all contracts and found this one to be eight years old and in many respects obsolete or inconsistent with the current legal climate and federal regulations, including Medicare.

Note: This implies he was not singled out unfairly.

4.2 Consistent with the implications of corporate responsibility that derived from the Darling case, the hospital's board of trustees now must have a mechanism to ensure the quality of all aspects of professional services in the institution, including ancillary departments such as pathology. The chief of this service has this responsibility and is corporately responsible to the board.

Note: It is hoped that this quick education on the Darling case will help set the stage for the chief's acceptance of the board's legal motivations and corporate responsibility for all medical practices in the hospital.

4.3 This is also consistent with the PSRO provisions of P.L. 92-603; and the hospital will have to provide its chairmen some kind of compensation to carry out quality monitoring and auditing functions as a *quid pro quo* for their efforts. Cite example of the physician coordinator of utilization review, who is on a part-time salary, and chief of rehabilitation medicine and E.R. medical director who are on full-time, salaried to carry out this medical quality control role.

Note: This may begin to establish the idea of fixed compensation in the pathologist's mind.

4.4 More specifically, the board is concerned over several recent court decisions that reaffirm the hospital's liability for all services provided by the laboratory including the professional services of the pathologists in accordance with the *Respondeat Superior* doctrine. Legally the hospital can no longer accept the "independent contractor" clause in the pathologist's current contract.

Note: This will further clarify the hospital's ultimate responsibility for professional services and may make the pathologist more receptive to the forthcoming argument that the hospital is also, therefore, ultimately responsible for regulating compensation arrangements and earnings and that the pathologists are part of the hospital's corporate structure, not independent of it.

4.5 Remind the chief pathologist of the hospital's commitment to the laboratory and the pathologists, *i.e.* the magnitude of capital expenditures, additions of new employees, and so on, over the past five years; all of which have helped the hospital and the pathologists provide the highest quality of services.

4.6 Then shift to the fact that our internal survey data reveal that the hospital's net margin in the laboratory is declining because the hospital is experiencing increased operating expenses for more staff, costlier supplies, and expensive capital purchases, to stay current with new technology, and that under our present contract the pathologist's professional compensation automatically adds proportionately to our costs — theirs being a variable cost to us because their compensation relates to gross revenues. If theirs was a fixed cost, as is true for most other employees, the hospital could offset increased supply and capital costs with the price increases.

Note: Again, the intent is to suggest fixed compensation for pathologists.

4.7 Reveal very disconcerting results from the areawide survey indicating that our laboratory charges are higher than those of neighboring hospitals, earnings are $25,000 more per F.T.E. pathologist than is true in other hospitals, annually our patients are paying a premium of about $70,000 more for laboratory services than patients in other hospitals are and that, as a consequence, our public vulnerability on this matter is very serious — so serious that we would have to admit our pathologists earn too much under the present open-ended arrangement and also that our patients are paying an unreasonable premium for these services. Point out that neither the hospital nor the pathologists would want to remain so publicly vulnerable as this. Cite the *Washington Post* and other media exposes — which have proved to be very embarrassing to the hospitals involved.

4.8 Do not conclude the first session with any specific recommendations that salary is the option we are thinking about — leave it obscure. The information should speak for itself.

4.9 Advise the chief pathologist that we have already spoken to the president of the medical staff and advised him that this is, and should be, a personal issue between administration and the pathologist and not subject to discussion at the medical executive committee or any other forum of the medical staff — because personal income is involved.

Note: This not only should make the chief pathologist aware that the president has been informed of the negotiations, but also suggests it is wise for both of us to keep it a closed issue — especially in view of the data just presented which let him know that we realize excessively high earnings are being made.

5. At the second meeting:

5.1 Bring up the inherent problems of open-ended contracts and, in particular, the percentage arrangements. Cite nationwide and local trends that indicate these plans are declining, while salaried arrangements are increasing. Cite the fact that other hospitals in the area are also contemplating such a change.

Note: This should help him hear the salary signals again and also make him feel that he is not the only pathologist to accept a salary.

5.2 Cite the fact that the 1970 Senate Anti-Trust and Monopoly Committee's hearings involved disclosures that only 10 percent of laboratory output relates to pathologists' direct involvement and consistent with this, it makes more sense for us to be talking about fixed compensation in relation to the quality monitoring and supervision function of the pathologists, and, therefore, is consistent with the decision set out in Sections 4.1 to 4.4.

5.3 Anticipate a defense on current earnings being comparatively high, including arguments that quality and range of services is higher here than at other hospitals. Refute the range of service argument based on survey data the hospital has that the pathologists' coverage, on-call and inhouse, is no greater than most hospitals.

5.4 Anticipate the argument that C.A.P. doesn't favor salaries. Respond with the fact that C.A.P. is not allowed to prohibit any pathologist from working under any agreement he chooses — per Justice Department consent decree in the late 1960's.

5.5 Anticipate several concessions, e.g. percentage of revenue with upper limits or sliding scale, etc.

5.6 Anticipate serious anxiety about what a salary would mean in terms of a cut in current earnings, especially the Chief's earnings. Don't resolve until he is more fully committed to go with a fixed compensation level.

5.7 Be prepared to raise questions about the qualifications of his junior partner, who is not yet Board Certified in both boards.

6. At the third meeting, hand the chief pathologist a proposed salary contract for himself and his two subordinates and leave actual dollar figures out and instead focus on the new

benefits they will receive: four weeks' vacation, paid educational leaves, sick time, malpractice liability coverage, annuity program, and others. Indicate the approximate value, e.g. "This is worth at least $20,000 to each of you." Then offer $90,000 for the chief based on areawide averages, *i.e.* $90,000 plus a minimum of $20,000 worth of benefits which amounts to a minimum value of $110,000. Expect this move to force him to focus his negotiation efforts on obtaining a $100,000 salary. Make this the bargaining range. Advise him that you are not authorized to approve this figure but will attempt to obtain it from the board if he is prepared to accept the offer at the next meeting.

D. Outcome:

After three meetings it became apparent to both the administrator and the chief pathologist that the chief pathologist was fast heading for a nervous breakdown. He resigned and left the hospital. His senior associate, who was not really qualified for the chief's role was offered it in an acting capacity, on a salary ($85,000), for a six month trial period, during which time we agreed not to interview other candidates until he proved he was or was not capable or interested in the position permanently.

As he had been earning $137,000 (and the chief had been earning $147,000 under the former contract) this $85,000 offer was so dramatic a cut for him that he resigned after two months. In other words, he apparently accepted the salary offer and acting role just so he would have time to look for another job. Before resigning, though, he agreed to request the College of American Pathologists' placement listings for the hospital (which can only be requested by the incumbent pathologists and not by administrators) and from this listing we were able to recruit a well trained East Coast pathologist within two months who was prepared to accept a $90,000 salary.

E. Actual Negotiations

What occurred during the negotiation process was that the chief pathologist had apparently been aware of his excessive compensation all along and came into the negotiations in a very anxious frame of mind because of his weak bargaining position. His personal share of the $344,000 was $147,000 and he could not see how the hospital was likely to sanction this as a salary. He had already made several moves to help deter what he knew was likely to happen.

For example, during the negotiations he made it clear that he wasn't getting the lion's share of the $344,000. He quickly pointed out that his senior partner was getting almost as much as he. He also implied he had made plans to hire a Ph.D. microbiologist soon — from his own income. He had contributed heavily to the hospital's building fund in the previous year, and presumably he felt all these efforts might minimize his being perceived as money hungry. He took a very strong position that it wasn't his fault that the hospital designed such a contract that gave him such high earnings.

There is no question that this became a tragic case where his own guilt about these earnings could not be relieved, because he also was trapped by the desire to retain them. It was interesting that during the negotiations the influence of his wife became apparent. He obviously had made his commitment to her. At the first meeting he conceded on several points, but by the second meeting he reversed his position on these points. This happened time and time again till the decision to go to a salary was forced in the third meeting with no option but to go home and reconsider. No fourth meeting was held and he never returned to the hospital.

7. Detailed Case Example

Renegotiating Percentage of Revenue Contract to Hospital-Regulated Combined Billing Contract

A. Initial Situation

In the middle 1970's, a newly appointed administrator at a 375 bed community hospital in the Northwest evaluated current professional earnings of his radiologists and pathologists; both groups were operating under percentage of gross revenue contracts. He discovered that five radiologists were earning $450,000.

The administrator undertook a confidential areawide survey of the nearest hospitals to determine if such contracts and levels of earnings were prevalent in the area. Again he discovered some initial resistance from neighboring administrators in providing their data. Again only the chief executives were involved in providing the data and they were assured of its anonymity, *i.e.* specific hospitals would not be listed in the survey results.

The study confirmed that the radiology contracts were yielding relatively higher earnings than was the case at most other hospitals even though percentage of gross was the commonest arrangement. Radiologists' earnings ranked third out of eight hospitals.

An internal survey confirmed that the radiology department was experiencing a gradual decline in profit margin — a result of increasing operational costs with no relief in the professional expenses. The department also had excessively high utilization rates (*i.e.* diagnostic procedures per day) compared with those of similar hospitals in a Blue Cross regional sampling.

The administrator presented these data to the chairman of the board of trustees, who in turn called an executive committee to discuss the findings. The administrator recommended that the contract be terminated and renegotiated.

B. Position — Objectives

In dealing with the radiology situation, the board's position was to end the present open-ended percentage of revenue arrangement and replace it with combined billing. It mandated two additional objectives: (1) the professional charges in the combined billing would be regulated by the hospital and (2) the hospital would have the ultimate authority to determine what amount of professional staffing was required in relation to volume of services provided by the department.

The reasoning for these objectives was as follows. Radiologists, unlike pathologists, may deserve variable compensation in relation to their work efforts and, therefore, a fixed compensation method would not be sought. However, to prevent the combined billing contract from yielding open-ended compensation to the radiologists (who would obviously have a financial incentive not to bring in a new partner until it became absolutely necessary), the hospital should have authority over professional staffing levels.

The hospital would also have to retain the right to regulate professional fees to prevent open-ended compensation through irresponsible fee escalations, or fee escalations based simply on areawide fees. The latter could develop because most neighboring hospitals continue to have percentage of revenue contracts and direct billing arrangements and areawide fees are escalating both in relation to the increasing charges (and, therefore, professional fees) at other hospitals and the vicious cycle of keeping up with each other.

C. Strategy

In this situation the same basic strategies were followed in the first four steps as were used in the previous case. In step 4 there were some minor differences because in that case the objective was to convert a percentage of gross contract to a straight salary.

In addition to these four steps, the following strategy was developed for the radiology situation:

1. Cite the 1965 A.C.R. directive that urged their membership to cease using revenue sharing arrangements.

2. When they have finally agreed to fee-for-service billing, rather than revenue sharing, anticipate resistance to combined billing and a strong move for direct billing. Cite additional costs of private collection efforts, ease and convenience for both parties if the hospital's business office does the billing, good public relations if patients receive only one bill, and fewer bad debts.

3. After they agree to combined billing, anticipate a strong move for total autonomy to determine their own charge structure. Cite the hospital's cost containment obligations, accountability to the public to ensure reasonable and fair fees by its hospital-based specialists and the high visibility that has resulted from abuses elsewhere, and the hospital's obligation to ensure that the total amount of the hospital component and the professional component is reasonable and does not escalate unreasonably.

4. Offer "concession" that hospital administration will not get into the business of determining professional charges *per se*. This prerogative will be left to the radiologists, provided they agree to develop their charge structure on an internally consistent base that the hospital can support if necessary: for example, a structure that allows twice the professional charge for a procedure that requires twice the professional time and involvement, in comparison to those of another procedure, and that all x-ray procedures should be so weighted.

5. To achieve this, suggest they use the California Relative Value Index or the A.C.R. Index and modify them as seems appropriate — but based only on professional work effort. The ultimate real objective is to get them onto a relative value index so administration can indirectly control aggregate professional charges by requiring the administration's annual approval of the dollar amount to be assigned to the basic unit.

Note: It is hoped that this move will make them feel that they are determining professional fees, even though the administration is ultimately controlling the total dollar value.

6. Anticipate resistance to this when the radiologists begin to see what it really might mean. Expect them to push for charges to be determined by market conditions, *i.e.* areawide

average professional fees for each procedure. Take a strong negative position if this is suggested, based on the difficulty of performing comprehensive annual surveys and the lack of availability of fee schedules from radiologists who bill directly, and most important, the hospital's public vulnerability if it merely sanctioned professional fees that might not have any real relation to professional work efforts.

7. Manifest the hospital's authority to regulate the required professional staffing on the basis that some abuses have already occurred in this department and the members are currently running with fewer F.T.E.'s than are other hospitals that handle equivalent volumes.

8. As a concession, be prepared to agree to fix the desired ratio of diagnostic interpretations per F.T.E. radiologist at the current level and that anything more than a 10 percent increase in volume (*i.e.* assuming there are five radiologists each handling roughly 20 percent of the department's volume) over the current level will warrant the addition of a sixth radiologist.

This says that even though your staff is currently handling more per man than other hospital radiologists, we will consider this a satisfactory quality of service and that future staffing will relate to this base year, with only a 10 percent volume variance before an addition is required. This should be acceptable to them as it allows the group to make 10 percent more income under the current arrangement, with probably no drop in income when another radiologist is brought on because initially he will be a junior partner receiving less compensation.

9. To establish a conversion from the present percent of gross arrangement to the new combined billing plan, make sure the radiologist's income is not reduced from its current level, which even though it is third out of eighth in the area is not unreasonably high. This will avoid further resistance to the change.

10. To accomplish this, propose that after the relative value scale is developed the administration will simply apply a dollar value to unit to yield aggregate current payments and, thereby, ensure that no loss of income occurs. Whatever dollar

value for the unit is arrived at in this way will serve as the first year's agreed upon unit amount and each year thereafter we will negotiate over this amount properly to take account of cost of living factors and other market conditions.

11. Expect the radiologists to make their own survey of area hospitals that use unit values and compare the results with the one they are being offered. If they are significantly lower, expect some bargaining to take place.

D. Outcome

All the desired objectives were achieved — a combined billing arrangement was agreed upon, relative value was the basis for charge determination, the hospital retained authority over the dollar amount applied to the unit value (which after it was worked out came to 80 cents per unit for the first year, even though this was about 20 cents per unit lower than the area averages). Also the hospital gained the authority to determine appropriate staffing levels, using the current year as the base level. The radiologists did not get a reduced compensation level during this transition.

Even though all objectives were accomplished, many strange things occurred in the process. The chief radiologist stepped down from his position and assumed a staff radiologist position four months after the negotiations (as a direct consequence of the negotiations), and the radiology department lost its nuclear medicine section, which subsequently allowed the hospital to negotiate a straight salary with the radiologist who assumed direction of nuclear medicine.

E. Actual Negotiations

The chief radiologist tried several delaying tactics, e.g. "I can't meet with you until I've met with my lawyer first"; "I can't give you an answer on that part of the contract until I speak to my associates, who are on vacation," and so on. He tried to get the chairman of the board to renege on several occasions.

Here is a hypothetical dialogue that shows how such a

negotiation might have gone: "Dr. Jones" is the chief radiologist, "Dr. Wilson" is one of his associates and "Mr. Bennett" is the administrator.

DR. JONES:

Mr. Bennett, you know that the American College of Radiologists favors percentage of gross arrangements, but they also very strongly recommend separate billing arrangements because they feel patients have a right to get a bill for services from the physician who provides the service.

MR. BENNETT:

Dr. Jones, I am aware of the ACR position and I respect it. However, let me first point out that they no longer recommend percentage of gross arrangements, but they do favor separate billing. I fully agree that our patients have a right to know what portion of a $100 x-ray bill relates to your component *versus* the costs related to the hospital's services. You and your 4 associates read each x-ray procedure and I think this should be known to the patient when he receives his bill. I don't think, however, that a separate direct bill to each patient from each radiologist is what we want to accomplish here.

I know also that you already got a quote from a private collection agency to handle your billing and this came to $60,000. This would be an extra $60,000 the public would have to be charged for you to recoup your extra costs . . . and I'm sure it's not your intention to have the public pay any more than absolutely necessary. I'd suggest the simplest and least expensive way is for us to do all your billing for you . . . at no extra cost to you or the public because we have to send a bill to every patient anyway. What we can also do is separate a "radiologist charge" out as distinguished from a hospital x-ray charge which I believe was the intent of the ACR recommendation for separate billing.

Also, I'm sure if you were a patient at this hospital you wouldn't want to be receiving a half a dozen different bills a couple of weeks after you were discharged.

DR. JONES:

Well, Mr. Bennett, I'm not saying that your proposal wouldn't be fair . . . I have always been committed to this hospital and I wouldn't have any problems with this change... I'm not trying to get rich off this hospital and our patients... but quite frankly, I don't think my 4 associates will find this acceptable. They'd prefer staying with our percentage of gross arrangement, but would only consider a direct billing arrangement as an alternative if they had to.

Note: Such comments by the Chief Radiologist could totally shift the entire negotiation process.

MR. BENNETT:

Dr. Jones...I'm afraid I must have been operating under a serious misunderstanding over these past two weeks...I was under the impression that you, as Chairman of the Department, were representing the 4 other radiologists...and I think I have tried to fairly and honestly answer all the questions they put forth to you...and that you, in turn, also conveyed back our position to them as we've been developing it...If you feel there is someone else among your associates who can represent them and get them to appreciate our problem and the need for a contract change, I'll be glad to meet with him personally...you've mentioned Dr. Wilson on several occasions; would you like me to negotiate this matter with him directly...in fact, I'd be willing to meet with all your associates and negotiate separate arrangements with each, if that's what you'd prefer.

Note: The Chief Radiologist picked up on the offer to have Dr. Wilson meet with me...but not without having him present because I think he sensed that his credibility as Chief would be further compromised. As a matter of fact, I think it is always dangerous to let a lower level subordinate go into binding negotiations...especially when he might gain a promotion by compromising in areas that his boss wouldn't compromise...especially if this pleased the people in a position to promote him. This is exactly the case that occurred in the next session even though Dr. Wilson was a much more aggressive negotiator. This session included, in addition to Dr. Jones, Dr. Wilson and Mr. Bennett, the chairman of the finance committee of the Board...primarily so Dr. Wilson would quickly see the Board was fully behind this contract change...

something it had taken Mr. Bennett four negotiating sessions to make clear to Dr. Jones and he didn't want to have to start at the beginning with a new radiologist.

Dr. Wilson got right to the point with the following statement:

DR. WILSON:

We have seen the data you gathered from neighboring hospitals and maybe this is correct, but I can tell you this . . . I know many radiologists who earn twice what we earn and I don't think our present percentage of gross arrangement is compensating us too much.

MR. BENNETT:

Fine, Dr. Wilson, you might be correct from what you hear in your cocktail circuit, but first let me say no one ever implied your compensation was too excessive . . . but rather that such open ended contracts are just no longer acceptable because they can result in inequitable compensation.

But if you're saying that you're not earning enough money under the present arrangement or the proposed new arrangement, let me remind you that if money is your sole motivation, we are still living in a free market . . . at least until the Rate Review Boards and Senate Subcommittees put an end to these arrangements . . . and if this were your sole motivation, I'd be the last to discourage you from going to the highest bidder. Obviously, I can only assume that other factors, other than compensation, are more important to you because you've clearly made a commitment to this hospital . . . But I can tell you this, and I'm sure the Board concurs, this hospital *will not* try to compete with any other hospital that might allow irresponsible arrangements that allow radiologists to earn twice or more what our radiologists earn . . . and I'm sure you wouldn't expect this Board and management to act irresponsibly.

Dr. Wilson was obviously a more aggressive negotiator, but he proved to be able to make commitments that his fellow radiologists accepted. The negotiating process moved much more quickly. It might be added that Dr. Wilson was more willing to make concessions than otherwise might be expected, given his good negotiating behavior. The reason was simply that he may have had his eyes on the chief's position and wanted administration's support when he made his move.

Such negotiations can be spread out over a long period. During that time, several other things could happen that probably relate to the chief's failure in the negotiations. Some staff radiologists could look for other jobs, some might begin to develop their own private radiology practice and there could be a move by a radiologist to break Nuclear Medicine out from the department of radiology. Such outcomes develop when the radiologists lose respect for their chief and if they do they significantly compromise his bargaining position with the administrator. For example, in one similar situation, the nuclear medicine physician gave very clear signals that for his independence as head of a free-standing department he would be prepared to negotiate a fixed compensation contract.

Another important thing can occur in the negotiations. In this hypothetical case, the contract terminated effective February 15 of that year. Since the negotiations were not complete, the administration agreed to make monthly payments to the radiologists based on 1/12th of the previous year's payments, even though volume was up from last year. This simple arrangement was continued until an agreement was reached. The negotiation process obviously goes faster with this implied threat of salary.

APPENDIX A
SAMPLE AREAWIDE SURVEY FORMAT

A. **EXPLANATIONS AND METHODOLOGY FOR COMPLETING SAMPLE AREAWIDE HOSPITAL-BASED SPECIALIST (H.B.S.) SURVEY:**

1. **Compensation Method:** This could include the following six basic arrangements:

1.1 Salary — This is a fixed payment either as an employee or non-payroll contract payments such as to an incorporated H.B.S.

1.2 Percent of Gross Charges — This simply means the H.B.S. receives a negotiated percentage of the gross billings of the department (frequently about 25% for Pathologists and 33% for Radiologists).

1.2.1 Simple Percent of Gross with routine deductions for allowances, discounts, etc.

1.2.2 Percent of Gross with Upper Limit

1.2.3 Percent of Gross with Sliding Scale (*i.e.* varying percent based on volume)

1.3 Percent of Net Income (with same subcategories as 1.2 above) — Like Percent of Gross, this simply means the H.B.S. receives a negotiated percent of his department's revenues, but with the additional proviso that it is based on the *net* revenue (or profits) of the department.

1.4 Fee-for-Service (based on relative value index or other means of charge determination). This simply refers to a payment per procedure, and what this fee is and who bills for it is subject to negotiation.

1.4.1 Direct Billing by H.B.S.

1.4.2 Combined Billing by Hospital.

1.5 Lease Arrangements — whereby the physician leases the space and/or equipment from the hospital and typically employs the technical staff himself. The hospital may or may not bill the patients on behalf of the H.B.S. in this arrangement.

1.6 Combinations of 1.1 through 1.5 above — This could, for example, include a basic salary to the Pathologist for all routine lab work plus a fee-for-service arrangement for all autopsies and surgical pathologies he has to perform and interpret.

2. **Department's Previous Year's Gross Revenue:** The desired figure here, for comparative purposes, is the total gross revenue or billings by the department, and in the case of radiology, it is more meaningful to gather this data in the following categories:

2.1 Gross Diagnostic (non-nuclear medicine) X-Ray Revenue.

2.2 Gross Radiation Therapy Revenue (if the department performs treatment services).

2.3 Gross Nuclear Medicine Revenue.

2.4 Other X-Ray Department Gross Revenues: This could include ultrasound and computerized axial tomography (C.A.T.) procedures.

N.B. As many hospitals do not provide radiation therapy services, these distinctions may help the data be more useful for comparative purposes. It can easily be argued that radiologist time in therapy is more extensive than the time expended for diagnostic interpretations. This data might also be valuable for negotiating 4 different types of contracts with the radiologists, representing their differential skills and involvement.

No such distinction in source of gross revenues is necessary for Pathology.

3. **Total Radiologist (or Pathologist) Compensation per Year:**
This is the total amount of payments (or deductions) the hospital has paid to its H.B.S.'s in a year's time. This is an easy figure to get from surrounding hospitals that utilize compensation arrangements 1.1, 1.2, 1.3, and 1.5 above. It may be relatively more difficult to get data on direct billing fee-for-service arrangements (1.4.1 above) because many hospitals may not have adequate data bases to obtain this information or the H.B.S. doesn't make his fee structure known to Administration. For one's own hospital, even if it's already on direct billing, this figure can be calculated if the hospital maintains any logs of the number of specific procedures (e.g. chest x-rays, angiograms, etc.) and has available the H.B.S. price structure.

4. **Average Professional Charge per Procedure:**
This column is important as indicator if the study hospital is significantly higher or lower than areawide professional charges. It is recommended that a sample of 10-20 benchmark procedures be used. The most difficult figures to get will be when direct billing is used. If Percent of Gross and Percent of Net is used the professional charge is easy to calculate. For example, if Hospital "A" and "B" both have a 33% of Gross arrangement

but Hospital "A" charges $10 for a routine chest X-Ray, while Hospital "B" charges $20 for the same procedure, their professional charges are $3.33 and $6.66 respectively. An average of 10 or 20 such comparable procedures will reveal any major variances in professional compensation.

5. **Total Professional Radiology (Pathology) Compensation per Bed:**
   This is a rough indicator of major variances in professional compensation on a "per bed" basis rather than a "per procedure" basis as in column 4 above. This is calculated simply by dividing column 3 by each hospital's total bed complement. The only limitation with this information is that some hospitals in the sample may have disproportionately more (or less) non medical/surgical beds (such as psychiatry beds) that will reveal a lower radiology or pathology professional cost per patient bed, simply because these beds require fewer such services. . .not because the professional component is lower. Also a hospital with low occupancy may show a low professional cost per bed, so this information can only be used as a rough substitute for a more detailed analysis like column 4.

6. **Actual Radiologist (Pathologist) Fees as Percentage of Gross:**
   This column is significant (even if the study hospital is not compensating on a Percent of Gross arrangement) because percentage of gross is the single most common arrangement with pathologists and radiologists. This column typically reveals that those hospitals on percent of gross arrangements are paying higher professional fees than hospitals under other arrangements; and in some cases salaried arrangements convert to only 10 or 15% of the department's gross revenues. This column is calculated simply by: Column 2 ÷ Column 3 × 100.

7. **Number of Full Time Equivalent Radiologists (Pathologists):**
This is frequently a difficult figure to get and the error is usually in upwards direction, *i.e.* a three man group of pathologists may claim that they are really equivalent to 3.5 because of vacation relief and sick relief coverage through moonlighting pathologists. A second problem is that a pathologist (or radiologist) may consider himself "full time" even though he may only put in 4 or 5 hours of work per day. Finally, the biggest problem is when a group of H.B.S.'s service more than one hospital; here it's almost impossible to find out what real coverage is provided. In any case, this information is critical because it might reveal a very high or low H.B.S. staffing pattern at one hospital versus the others.

8. Average Annual Compensation per Radiologist (or Pathologist):
The actual income per man would be rarely known for sure, because the Chief Radiologist or Pathologist may not be willing to reveal what he actually pays his associates. This is not critical, but rather what the average compensation per specialist is, for comparative purposes. For example, if Hospital "A" has 3 Full Time Equivalent Pathologists (per No. 7 above) and paid total pathologist compensation of $150,000 last year (per No. 3 above), the average compensation per man is $50,000. If the study hospital had 6 Full Time Equivalent Pathologists and paid $600,000 (per No. 3 above), this obviously means $100,000 per man, and this difference is significant.

B. INTERPRETING SURVEY RESULTS:

Comparing the averages of all areawide hospitals, column by column, with the Study Hospital ("Community Medical Center") could reveal the following:

1. If the Study Hospital has a higher average professional charge per procedure (column No. 4), this could mean:

    1.1 Study Hospital is allowing excessive professional charges because of high personal compensation demands by H.B.S.'s.

    1.2 Study Hospital is supporting more H.B.S.'s than other hospitals and this extra staff is reflected in higher professional costs. To check this out (vs. option B-1.1), look at column 7 or column 8.

    1.3 If the Study Hospital is on a Percent of Gross or Net, the higher than average professional compensation may simply relate to the hospital's higher than average total charge for x-ray or laboratory procedures, which, in turn, is reflected in higher professional compensation. This can be confirmed by a benchmark analysis of common procedure charges at neighboring hospitals.

2. If the Study Hospital has a higher than average professional compensation (based on 10-20 benchmark procedures) per bed compared with other hospitals, it could mean:

    2.1 The Study Hospital has a higher occupancy of its beds than the average of other hospitals in the survey.

    2.2 The Study Hospital has a relatively higher proportion of medical/surgical beds than other hospitals in the survey.

    2.3 The Study Hospital performs significantly more outpatient radiology (or lab) services.

    2.4 Or, the same possibilities as noted above in B-1.1, 1.2 and 1.3

3. If the Study Hospital has a higher "average annual compensation per radiologist (or pathologist)" than the average of other hospitals in the survey, this could mean:

   3.1 All the possibilities listed in B-1.1, 1.2 and 1.3 above.

   3.2 Relatively fewer radiologists (or pathologists) are being employed at the Study Hospital compared to other hospitals in the survey. For example, if Hospital "A" retains four radiologists at a cost of $400,000 this means $100,000 per man; while the Study Hospital may retain only two radiologists for roughly the same volume of services (and total compensation paid), but this would yield an average annual compensation of $200,000 per man. Although in most cases tight staffing might be desirable, a radiologist who attempts to read too many films will only end up compromising the quality of his interpretations to obtain greater personal income.

4. If the Study Hospital has a lower "average compensation per radiologist (or pathologist)" than the average of other hospitals in the survey, this could mean:

   4.1 The professional charge structure is low.

   4.2 Too many radiologists or pathologists are being retained by the hospital. Six pathologists handling roughly the same volume of work as three pathologists at another hospital would yield data implying average pathologist compensation in the former case was relatively low while this might only be an indication of greater inefficiency (or less actual work time) by pathologists in the former hospital. It could also be an indication that the Chief Pathologist is retaining several low salaried associates and his personal income is significantly higher. The acid test would be to look at column No. 4 which would reveal higher professional charges per procedure, even though the average compensation per pathologist might be low by comparison. Also, another way to determine if an excessive number of pathologists or radiologists are being retained:

4.2.1 For radiologists: compare total number of diagnostic x-rays per full time equivalent radiologist at Study Hospital; if the radiologists are performing less than the 14,000 interpretations per year recommended by the American College of Radiology, it may be overstaffed.

4.2.2 Pathologist: The only rough indicator to excessive pathologist staffing is to compare number of Full Time Equivalent Pathologists per bed at Study Hospital versus this same figure for other survey hospitals. One caution relates to the fact that a hospital with a very low surgical load obviously requires few surgical pathologies and, therefore, may need fewer pathologists. The second factor relates to volume of outpatient laboratory work; a hospital with significantly more than 20 percent of its laboratory work coming from outpatient referrals will require more F.T.E. pathologists per bed than a hospital with lower outpatient laboratory work.

5. If the study hospital's average annual compensation per radiologist and pathologist was $150,000 or more, these radiologists and pathologists were earning more than 85 percent of other radiologists and pathologists based on a nationwide study (per a 1975-1977 survey by the Health Care Financing Administration of the Department of Health Education and Welfare).

SAMPLE AREA WIDE HOSPITAL-BASED PHYSICIAN SURVEY — RADIOLOGY

	(1) Compensation Method	(2) Department's Previous Year's Gross Revenue	(3) Total Radiologist Compensation/ Year	(4) Average Professional Charge per Procedure	(5) Total Professional Radiology Compensation Per Bed	(6) Actual Radiologist Fees as Percent of Gross	(7) Number of Full Time Equivalent Radiologists	(8) Average Annual Compensation per Radiologist
Hospital "A"								
Hospital "B"								
Hospital "C"								
Hospital "D"								
Hospital "E"								
Hospital "F"								
Hospital "G"								
Hospital "H"								
Community Medical Center (Study Hospital)								
All Hospitals Average								

SUGGESTED READINGS

Chapter I The Issues

1. Overview

American Hospital Association Guidelines: *Contractual Relationships Between Hospitals and Physicians,* American Hospital Association, Chicago, 1976.

"The Quiet Issue of What Hospitals Pay Pathologists Is Getting Noisier" *Modern Hospital,* June 1970, 94-105.

"Medicine's New Royalists", Editorial; *Detroit Free Press,* Feb. 4, 1973.

"Pathologist: More. . .Making $200,000 a Year", Editorial Series, *Washington Post,* Nov. 1, 1972.

"Ralph Nader vs. The Hospitals", Editorial, *Chicago Tribune,* Aug. 16, 1977.

Morell, James and Rogan, Peter, "Hospital-Based Physician Compensation Concepts", *Topics in Health Care Financing,* Vol. 4, No. 3 (Spring, 1978), 11-26.

Letourneau, Charles, M.D., *The Hospital Medical Staff,* Starling Publications, Chicago, 1964.

Penn, Robert, "Negotiating with Your Professionals", *Hospital Financial Management,* October 1968.

2. Financial Impact

Final Report: Study of Reimbursement and Practice Arrangements of Provider-Based Physicians, Department of Health, Education and Welfare, Health Care Financing Administration, Dec. 1977; H.E.W. Contract No. 600-76-0055.

College of American Pathologists Manual of Ethical and Contractual Relationships, Chicago, Illinois 1962.

3. Economic Implications

Leftwich, Richard, "The Price System and Resource Allocation", Holt, Rinehart and Winston, Feb. 1965.

Hospital Law Manual, Health Law Center, Pittsburgh, Pennsylvania.

Ludlam, James, "Legal Pitfalls in Exclusive Physician-Hospital Agreements", *The Hospital Medical Staff* (American Hospital Association), Dec. 1975, 6-10.

Adler v. Montefiore Hospital Association of Western Pennsylvania (1973), 311, A.2d 634.

Blank v. The Palo Alto-Stanford Hospital Center (1965), 234, C.A. 2d 377.

Datillo v. Tucson General Hospital, 533 P.2d 700.

Rush v. City of St. Petersburg, 205, So. 2d 11 (Florida Court of Appeals 1967).

"The Quiet Issue of What Hospitals Pay Pathologists is Getting Noisier", *Modern Hospital,* June 1970, 94-105.

A Guide for Radiologists in Relationships with Institutions, American College of Radiology, Chicago, Illinois, 1961.

Manual of Ethical and Contractual Relationships, College of American Pathologists, Chicago, Illinois, 1962.

Somers, Herman and Anne, *Medicare and the Hospitals — Issues and Perspectives,* The Brookings Institution, Washington, D.C., 1967.

Hospital Week, Vol. 15 No. 26 (June 29, 1979) "U.S. Judge Clears Anesthesiology Society for Anti-Trust Charge Involving Guide."

4. *Impact of Cost Reimbursement and Regulated Rate Setting*

Final Report: Study of Reimbursement and Practice Arrangements of Provider-Based Physicians, Department of Health, Education and Welfare, Health Care Financing Administration, Dec. 1977, H.E.W. Contract No. 600-76-0055.

Head, James Jr., "Regulatory Environment for Physician Compensation", *Topics in Health Care Financing,* Vol. 4, No. 3 (Spring 1978), 75-90.

5. *Medicare Impact*

Somers, Herman and Anne, *Medicare and the Hospitals — Issues and Perspectives,* The Brookings Institution, Washington, D.C., 1967.

"A.M.A. Sticks to Its Reservations About Medical Care at Clinical Meeting", Special Report, Trustee (American Hospital Association), Feb. 1967, 19-22.

Van Dyke, Frank, Hospital-Based Specialist Study: Pathologists and Radiologists Arrangements with Hospitals, 1965-1968, Columbia University School of Public Health.

"Separate Billing From Hospitals Now College Policy", *American College of Radiology Bulletin,* Oct. 15, 1965.

"Medicare Changes Relationships — A.C.R. Suggests Sample Hospital-Radiologist Agreement/College Studies Separate Billing Arrangements", *American College of Radiology Bulletin Pre-Print,* Nov. 1965.

"Hospital-Based Medical Specialists and S.3205", President's Letter, American Hospital Association, Sept. 1976.

Statement of the College of American Pathologists on the Preliminary Proposed Regulations for Reimbursement Under Medicare For Services of Hospital-Based Physicians, Feb. 11, 1966.

6. *Ethics of Medical Economics*

Opinions and Reports of the Judicial Council, American Medical Association, Chicago, Illinois, 1972.

Speech by Wesley Hall, M.D., Chairman of A.M.A.'s Board of Trustees overruling A.M.A.'s House of Delegates' "ethical" boycott resolution, *Group Health and Welfare News,* Sept. 1966, p. 8.

Reals, William J., M.D., "Contractual Arrangements Between Physicians and Hospitals — A Physician's View", *The Hospital Medical Staff,* Vol. 6, No. 2 (Feb. 1977), 1-5.

7. *Corporate Practice of Medicine Issue*

Somers, Herman and Anne, *Doctors, Patients and Health Insurance,* Brookings Institution, Washington, D.C., 1961.

Letourneau, Charles, M.D., *The Hospital Medical Staff,* Starling Publication, Chicago, Illinois, 1964.

Journal of the American Medical Association 84 (July 17, 1925) A.M.A.'s position in support of radiologist interpretations as the practice of medicine.

Journal of the American Medical Association 112 (May 27, 1939) A.M.A.'s position supporting the practice of pathology as the practice of medicine.

Hospital Accreditation References, American Hospital Association, 1957 — the J.C.A.H. denies x-ray, EKG and pathological interpretations as consultations.

Sausser v. Department of Health of the City of New York, 150 N.E. 603.

Maranville v. State Board of Equalization, 222 P. 2d 898.

Travelers Insurance Company v. Bergeron 25F 2d 680.

8. *The Independent Contractor and Respondeat Superior Issue*

"Questions and Answers — The Emergency Department Physician Staff: Independent or Hospital-Employed", J.A.M.A., Volume 235, No. 21 (May 24, 1976).

Darling v. Charleston Community Memorial Hospital, 33 Ill. 2d 326, 211 N.E. 2d 253 (1965).

Hodges v. Doctors Hospital, 234 S.E. 2d, 116 (Georgia, 1977).

Gonzales v. Nork and Mercy Hospital of Sacramento, Superior Court No. 228-566, Sacramento County (1973).

Keene v. Methodist Hospital, 234 F. Supp. 233 (1971, Indiana).

Beeck v. Tucson General Hospital, 500 P. 2d 1153, Arizona Court of Appeals, 1972.

Mduba v. Benedictine Hospital, 384 N.Y.S. 2d 527 (Appellate Division 1976).

Snelson v. Margaretville Hospital, N.Y.S. 2d 579 (Appellate Division 1975).

Mehlman v. Powell, 47 U.S.L.W. 2227 (Maryland, October 28, 1977).

"Examination of the Contract Relationships Between Hospitals and Hospital-Based Physicians," May 10, 1979, presentation to the National Health Lawyers Association by Philip Flame of Flame, Sanger, Grayson, and Ginsburg.

9. *Professional Status Issue*

"Medicare Changes Relationships — A.C.R. Suggest Sample Hospital-Based Radiologist Agreement/College Studies Separate Billing Arrangements", *American College of Radiology Bulletin Pre-Print,* November 1965.

"Radiologists Seek 'Same Basis as Other Physicians'", *A.C.R. Bulletin,* October 15, 1965.

"The Emergency Physician — A New Specialist Moves Into the 'Pit'", *Medical World News,* Volume 15, No. 5 (February 1, 1974).

Satillaro, Anthony, M.D., "An Open Approach to Contractual Arrangements", *The Hospital Medical Staff,* Volume 7, No. 3 (March 1978).

10. Direct Billing

Special Report on Fee-For-Service, Direct Billing, Pennsylvania Insurance Department, 1974.

"Independent Practice Supported by Blue Shield Executive", *A.C.R. Bulletin,* March 1975.

Final Report: Study of Reimbursement and Practice Arrangements of Provider-Based Physicians, Department of Health, Education and Welfare, Health Care Financing Administration, December 1977, H.E.W. Contract No. 600-76-0055.

Chapter II Hospital-Based Physicians — Their Position

Blakely, R.M., "Hospital Physicians: How They Are Paid and How Much", *Modern Hospital* 121 (August 1973).

A Guide for Radiologists, American College of Radiology, Chicago, Illinois, 1977.

Kraus, W. A., "New Threat to Fee-For-Service", *Impact,* May 24, 1976.

Mathews, F., "Contracts with Hospitals", *Medical Economics* 50 (June 25, 1973).

Reals, William J., M.D., "Contractual Arrangements Between Physicians and Hospitals — A Physician's View, *The Hospital Medical Staff,* Vol. 6, No. 2 (February 1977).

Letourneau, Charles, M.D., *Hospital Medical Staff,* Starling Publications, Chicago, Illinois 1964.

Webb, Samual and Fenhagen, Henry "Full Time Emergency Department Physicians", *The Hospital Medical Staff,* Volume 2, No. 7 (July 1973).

Statement of Policy, American Society of Anesthesiologists, Chicago, Illinois, January 1963.

Beecher, Henry K., "Trends in Anesthesia", *J.A.M.A.* 180:1 (April 7, 1962).

Washmuth, C. E., *Anesthesia and the Law,* C. C. Thomas, Springfield, Illinois, 1961.

"Emergency Room Physician Guarantees" Special Release, Director of Financial Management, American Hospital Association, February 1975.

Accreditation Manual for Hospitals — Anesthesia Services/Principles, April 1976, 59-61.

Accreditation Manual for Hospitals — Nuclear Medicine Services/Principles, April 1976, 117-120.

Accreditation Manual for Hospitals — Pathology Services, April 1976, 135-140.

Accreditation Manual for Hospitals — Physical Medicine Services, April 1976, 149-151.

Accreditation Manual for Hospitals — Respiratory Care Services, April, 1976, 161-164.

Kessler, Marian S. "Physician Compensation Survey Shows Marked Increase in Contractual Arrangements", *The Hospital Medical Staff,* Volume 5, No. 7 (July 1976).

Lewin v. St. Joseph Hospital of Orange, 82 Cal. App. 3d 368 (1978).

Chapter III Hospitals — Their Position

"Medicine's New Royalists", Editorial — *Detroit Free Press,* February 4, 1973.

Sutton, Frank, M.D. "Developing Workable Relationships with Hospital-Based Specialists", *Trustee,* Volume 23, No. 6 (June 1970).

Regan, William, "Executive Director and Contract Physicians", *Regan Report on Hospital Law,* Volume 15, No. 12 (April 1975).

Halonen, R. J. and Norville, J.L., "Contracting with Hospital-Based Physicians: The Administrator's Role" *Hospital Progress* 57 (November 1976).

Halonen R. J. and Norville, J. L., "Negotiating and Administering Contracts with Hospital-Based Physicians", *Hospital Progress* 56 (June 1975).

Hitt, D. H., "Contractual Arrangements Between Physicians and Hospitals — An Administrator's View", *The Hospital Medical Staff* 6 (February 1977).

Darling v. Charleston Community Memorial Hospital, 33 Ill., 2d 326, 211 N.E. 2d 253 (1965).

Gonzales v. Nork and Mercy Hospital of Sacramento, Superior Court No. 228-566, Sacramento County (1973).

American Hospital Association Guidelines: Contractual Relationships Between Hospitals and Physicians, American Hospital Association, Chicago, 1976.

Chapter IV Bystanders to the Negotiation Process

Health Research Group "Public Citizen", News Release, Washington, D.C., August 11, 1977.

"Pathologists: More. . .Making $200,000 a Year", Editorial Series, *Washington Post,* November 1, 1972.

"Ralph Nader vs. The Hospitals", Editorial, *Chicago Tribune,* August 16, 1977.

"Medicine's New Royalists", Editorial, *Detroit Free Press,* February 4, 1973.

Chapter V Prospects for a Final Resolution

National Steering Committee on Voluntary Cost Containment, Joint Statements by A.H.A., A.M.A., F.A.H. — December 12, 1977.

American Hospital Association "Physician's Remuneration Has Impact on Hospital Costs", Hospitals, J.A.H.A. Volume 51, No. 15 (August 1, 1977).

Nierenberg, Gerard, The Art of Negotiating — Psychological Strategies For Gaining Advantageous Bargains, Cornerstone Library Publication, New York, 1971.

Chapter VI Negotiating Process

Schelling, Thomas, *The Strategy of Conflict,* Oxford University Press, New York 1960.

Nierenberg, Gerard, *The Art of Negotiating,* Cornerstone Library Publications, New York, 1971.

Coffin, Royce, *Negotiation, A Manual for Winners.*

Nash, J. F., "The Bargaining Problem", *Econometrica,* Volume 18, 155-162.

Luce, R. Duncan and Raiffer, Howard, *Games and Decisions,* New York, 1957.

Rodell, Fred, *Woe Unto You, Lawyers,* Pageant Press, New York, 1957.

Korda, M., *Power! How to Get It, How to Use It,* Random House, New York, 1975.

Ringer, R. J., *Winning Through Intimidation,* Los Angeles Book Publishers Company, Los Angeles, 1973.

Medical Economics Continuing Survey, *Medical Economics*.

Berne, Erik, *Games People Play*.

Chapter VII Negotiating Strategies and Tactics

Laubach, Peter; Laubach, Paul; Eaves, William and Rand, Richard, *Process, Art and Technique of Negotiating*, American College of Hospital Administrators, EMSCO, 1977.

Nierenberg, Gerard, *The Art of Negotiating*, Cornerstone Library Publications, New York, 1971.

Schelling, Thomas, *The Strategy of Conflict*, Oxford University Press, New York 1960.

Lee, Irving, L., "Procedure for Coercing Agreement", Harvard Business Review, January-February 1954.

Von Neumann, J., and Morgenstern, O., *Theory of Games and Economic Behavior*, Princeton, 1953.

Nash, J. F. "Two Person Cooperative Game", *Econometrica*, Volume 21 (1953).

Deutsch, Morton, "Trust and Suspicion", *The Journal of Conflict Resolution* 2:265-279 (December 1958).

Index

-A-

-B-

-C-

-D-

-E-

-F-

-R-